What people are

Mystical A

John C. Robinson's *Mystical Activism* is a powerful introduction to spiritual consciousness for those who have thought that religion is either for the empty-headed or for the reactionary, and a compelling challenge to those whose spiritual or mystical experiences have so absorbed them that they have little interest in social transformation.

Rabbi Michael Lerner, editor of Tikkun.org and author of 12 books, most recently *Revolutionary Love: A Political Manifesto to Heal and Transform the World* (University of California Press, 2019)

Mystical Activism is a book that is urgently needed in this time of environmental and cultural crisis, reminding us that frightening statistics and apocalyptic predictions are not enough – that the wisdom and will that can save our planet can only come from deep experience of the sacredness of life on Earth. This book is a beautiful, practice-filled guide to accessing mystical consciousness and committing to using the soul gifts we find there in service to a world teetering on a knife's edge between collapse and transformation.

Ron Pevny, Director of the Center for Conscious Eldering and author of *Conscious Living, Conscious Aging*

John C. Robinson's *Mystical Activism: Transforming a World in Crisis* is a book for a world and a people living in an apocalyptic age – an age of destruction and revelation, of despair and opportunity. It recognizes that such times require more than mere political activism; they require a spiritual transformation as well. Robinson offers the reader practical steps for this transformation, presenting tools for us to come home – a spiritual "Odyssey" if you will – to a more grounded and present awareness of our place in the world. It is truly a book for our time.

Theodore Richards, author of *The Great Re-imagining* and *A Letter to My Daughters* and Founder of The Chicago Wisdom Project

Mystical Activism: Transforming a World in Crisis is a call for all people to rise up to our next level of active spirituality and intergenerational mutuality. Never before has it been so important that the human species dives deep into our inner world so that we may draw forth our divinity and act in a way that can positively transform our world in crisis. Every religion began as a mystical experience; in this book Robinson challenges us to see the world from this divine knowing as sacred, cosmic beings all interconnected and interdependent so that we might begin again while drawing upon ancient wisdom. Interweaving science with spirituality, Robinson is doing what is especially vital at this time – calling upon us all to create new mythologies, narratives, and wisdom stories that will guide us toward universal healing and cooperation as well as a return to sacred living. Inspiring, moving and challenging in all the right ways, *Mystical Activism* is a guidebook for saving our world.

Rev. Deshna Charron Ubeda, Interfaith Minister and Chaplain, Director of ProgressiveChristianity.org and ProgressingSpirit. com

"Walk the mystical path with practical feet," the noted cultural anthropologist Angeles Arrien would reply when asked how to live well. This an excellent how-to-guide to do just that! John Robinson, using a clear model based in perennial wisdom and modern psychology, guides us through inviting exercises, clear examples and daily practices to support a healthy existence for ourselves and the planet. This is a wonderful resource for claiming greater happiness and our innate roles as both mystics and activists.

Deidre Combs, DMin, Combs and Company: Cross Cultural Consulting on Conflict Resolution, and author of *The Way of Conflict*; *Worst Enemy, Best Teacher*; and *Thriving Through Tough Times*

Mystical Activism is a heartfelt guide to healing that integrates psychological insight and spiritual depth. John Robinson writes with the seasoned clarity that comes from decades of experience as a psychotherapist and spiritual elder while approaching the mystical journey with a beginner's mind. *Mystical Activism* is written with the understanding that the healing of self and world are one and the same and needed now more than ever!

Skylar Wilson, founder: Wild Awakenings, co-author of *Order of the Sacred Earth: An Intergenerational Vision of Love and Action*

John Robinson's *Mystical Activism* is a practical and profound guide for those seeking to link their inner spiritual life with their concerns for our crisis-ridden world. Robinson argues for a radical kind of activism that flows spontaneously from the thought-free consciousness of mystical awareness. Maintaining that the ecological crisis of climate change is creating an evolutionary pressure for a collective awakening, Robinson outlines a practical path to allow us to participate in this profound unfolding. Passionate, inspiring, and wise.

David Nicol, the Subtle Activism Network, author of *Subtle Activism: The Inner Dimension of Social and Planetary Transformation*

Mystical
Activism

Transforming a World in Crisis

Mystical Activism

Transforming a World in Crisis

John C. Robinson

Foreword by Matthew Fox

CHANGEMAKERS
BOOKS

Winchester, UK
Washington, USA

JOHN HUNT PUBLISHING

First published by Changemakers Books, 2020
Changemakers Books is an imprint of John Hunt Publishing Ltd., No. 3 East Street,
Alresford, Hampshire SO24 9EE, UK
office@jhpbooks.com
www.johnhuntpublishing.com
www.changemakers-books.com

For distributor details and how to order please visit the 'Ordering' section on our website.

Text copyright: John C. Robinson 2018

ISBN: 978 1 78904 418 8
978 1 78904 419 5 (ebook)
Library of Congress Control Number: 2019941485

A CIP catalogue record for this book is available from the British Library.

Design: Stuart Davies

UK: Printed and bound by CPI Group (UK) Ltd, Croydon, CR0 4YY
US: Printed and bound by Thomson-Shore, 7300 West Joy Road, Dexter, MI 48130

We operate a distinctive and ethical publishing philosophy in
all areas of our business, from our global network of authors to
production and worldwide distribution.

Contents

Previous Books

Death of a Hero, Birth of the Soul: Answering the Call of Midlife
1571780432
But Where Is God? Psychotherapy and the Religious Search
1560725046
Ordinary Enlightenment: Experiencing God's Presence in Everyday Life 0871592614
Finding Heaven Here 1846941566
The Three Secrets of Aging: A Radical Guide 1780990408
Bedtime Stories for Elders: What Fairy Tales Can Teach Us About the New Aging 1780993539
What Aging Men Want: The Odyssey as a Parable of Male Aging
1780999814
Breakthrough 1785350924
The Divine Human: The Final Transformation of Sacred Aging
1780992365

This book is gratefully dedicated to Matthew Fox, the renowned teacher, activist and advocate of Creation Spirituality.

Awakening our original religious impulse, Creation Spirituality seeks to replace the dogma of the patriarchy with the reverent awareness of the sacred Earth. Rejoining psyche and cosmos, Heaven and Earth, human and divine, masculine and feminine, mystic, artist, prophet and scientist, Creation Spirituality urges all of us to transform ourselves, our work, and our civilization before it is too late.

Foreword by Matthew Fox

John Robinson identifies as a psychologist, interfaith minister, mystic and writer on conscious aging. In this book he wears all those hats and more. Bringing them together he lights a fire to our hearts, minds and souls and offers deep medicine for our struggling times, times he is unafraid to recognize as an "approaching apocalypse." John has his feet squarely on the ground and his heart, soul and spirit soaring. He also invites the rest of us to soar – soaring is another word for mysticism, for stretching our boundaries and expanding our consciousness.

He is on to something. Something primal and important seems to have been lost. Something triggered by the deepfelt awe and reverence and gratitude that our earliest ancestors must have felt amidst the wonder and the challenges they faced daily in a world of sparkling stars and dark skies, awesome land creatures and vast plains and forests, pure rivers and boundless oceans. The late mystic-priest-scientist Teilhard de Chardin named this experience as the "cosmic sense." This is how he put it:

> I give the name of cosmic sense to the more or less confused affinity that binds us psychologically to the All which envelops us... The cosmic sense must have been born as soon as humanity found itself facing the frost, the sea and the stars. And since then we find evidence of it in all our experience of the great and unbounded: in art, in poetry, and in religion.[1]

This rich book, born of Robinson's own deeply felt intuition around the "All that envelops us" amidst a sense of the "unbounded," rings true and sings to our hearts. For good reason then does Robinson begin his book with an excellent and moving telling of the new creation story – by beginning with the "All" he lets us know that he is offering us a post-modern way to explore the soul and society. With context, not text. With the "sacred ground of Creation" that has gradually been lost in an ever increasingly anthropocentric (what Pope Francis has called "narcissistic") world view. What the author calls "The World of Man" so preoccupied the modern era in the West, that it slowly banished the world of the sacred. The context of the universe and its story precedes all other sacred texts by about 13.7 billion years after all. Creation precedes Bibles just as "praise precedes faith" (Rabbi Heschel).

This book, beginning with its first chapter and building throughout, expands the heart. It is in the heart after all that our pre-modern ancestors believed truth resided (not in the head). For example, Thomas Aquinas, who was as hefty an intellectual as Western civilization has ever produced, said simply, "the proper objects of the heart are truth and justice." In this he is echoing the wisdom of Judaism that also places truth in the heart and not the head. The modern age, on the other hand, put truth in the head and some remnants of that era, those who identify as scientific materialists today, actually put consciousness itself in the brain. British scientist Rupert Sheldrake exposes the folly in such efforts.[2] The Enlightenment and modern era's bias against mysticism is well attested to. Theodore Roszak, one of the pioneers of Ecopsychology, reminded us that, "the Enlightenment held mysticism up for ridicule as the worst offense against science and reason." John Robinson is taking on the powers of Enlightenment thinking and education and religion and even psychology in this book. Far from ridiculing mysticism he in fact recommends it as much needed medicine for our excessively rational and unhappy times. His medicine heals a too-rational approach to life and thinking that feeds patriarchy but is killing our souls and the Earth and raising havoc on children and the future, on women and ultimately on men as well.

If the work of the prophet is to "interfere," as Rabbi Heschel teaches, then Robinson is indeed playing a prophetic role in this book. He interferes with our excessively rational approach to life and to superficial religion by telling us of his experience of coming out of the closet as a mystic and inviting others to do the same. Robinson is to be commended for his courage in coming out of the closet as a mystic. How many others have exhibited that courage? This book offers a fine testimony of what is at stake and how persons and culture itself can be healed when mystics speak out.

Robinson is explicit about interfering with a patriarchy that is killing the planet and that, in Adrienne Rich's keen observation, is serving up a "fatalistic self-hatred" for all to indulge in. How else can one explain denial of climate change for example at the highest places in American government and in an entire political part in America than by a "fatalistic self-hatred"? Who can ever again believe parents or grandparents who say they love their children and grandchildren while denying climate change and refusing to act to stop it?

Robinson revealed a prophetic role previously where in 1999 he took on his own profession and called for a "responsible integration of psychotherapy and spirituality," pointing out that conventional psychotherapy completely missed the mystical dimension of healing. In my book on *The Reinvention of Work* I insisted that that was the role all awakened people must play in their professions: To call them to their deeper truths, to assist their genuine service, to infiltrate if necessary to bring the spiritual back to our work worlds. Robinson has done that in his profession. Other graduates of our University of Creation Spirituality have done the same, including Bernard Amadei who went back to his school of engineering and launched Engineers Without Borders which now hosts over 18,000 members, who are busy bringing the gifts of solar generated irrigation wells and other miracles engineers offer us to countries including Afghanistan and Haiti, places in Africa and the Amazon.

Educators have done the same by incorporating our well tested pedagogy of instructing both right and left hemisphere learning into programs and schools for adults and for teenagers.

Robinson also interferes with the often secularized version of aging that still dominates much of the literature and practice of growing old. He challenges any version of aging that leaves out the mystical awakening that happens as we move beyond institutional work worlds and grow older. A fuller expression of our mysticism (what Einstein called our "intuition" from which values derive) can happen if we provide the awareness and the tools for that special rite of passage.

In this book Robinson summarizes many of these acts of interference in a fresh and vivid way. But he does not stop there. He also offers many practices that can get the heart opening and the mystic returning and the heart aflame no matter what our age or station in life. He is walking his talk and talking his walk for he shares with us his own story of his unfolding as a mystic and offers ways by which we can do the same.

A good example of a practice that can be very fruitful is his invitation to create a dialogue with the soul or the "right brain" which he sees as an "open door to the realms of the spirits." He shares with us some of his own dialogues and instructs us in how we can create our own. Rightly does he propose that we "don't have a goal. Just wake up." This is Meister Eckhart's teaching – and that of many Buddhist teachers as well – that we learn to live and work "without a why." The goal is less important than the process. We are told to "stand still and become one with... a bench... a blackberry bush... water... become it, just as it is... When you stand still and become pure silence and wonder, transparent to the beings and energies of what is, then you're home."

Robinson takes on one of the scourges of modern consciousness which is an explosion of patriarchy with its world of untold privileges and power-over tactics. By encouraging the development of our right brains or mystical capacities he is undercutting much of patriarchy just as feminist theologian Dorothee Soelle explained when she wrote that mysticism "comes closest to overcoming the hierarchical masculine concept of God... The mystical certainty that nothing can separate us from the love of God grows when we ourselves become one with love by placing ourselves, freely and without guarantee of success, on the side of love."[3] She insists that "the language of religion, by which I do not mean the stolen language in which a male God ordains and imperial power radiates forth, is the language of mysticism: I am completely and utterly in God, I cannot fall out of God, I am imperishable. 'Who shall separate us from the love of God?' we can then ask with Paul the mystic: 'neither death nor life, height nor depth, neither present nor future' (Romans 8:35 and 38)."[4] In other words, to stand up for mysticism is to stand up for a feminist consciousness and for deconstructing a destructively patriarchal view of the world.

Robinson also instructs us in the real and healthy masculine by exegeting the story of Odysseus, a story he finds to be especially relevant to today's situation because "the World of Man is a fundamentally patriarchal structure... maintained by men, it is not inclined toward mysticism." It bears within it the "values of ingrained warrior masculinity – men acting synergistically modeling and reinforcing patterns of nonnegotiable strength, self-sufficiency, reactive aggression, and submission to the alpha male hierarchy." Such toxic masculinity brings about psychological harm with vast social implications trapping men "in narrow, emotion-constricting roles as well as harming women, indigenous peoples, animals and the Earth herself." He sees in *The Odyssey* a relevant myth that tells us how to "come home from the warrior life of the patriarchy" and the wisdom that comes as Odysseus (and we) mature. In all this Robinson offers an important critique of patriarchy but also medicine for moving to a healthier place.

This book abounds with wise teachings about the most

important issues of our time. It is a book that promises transformation of a deep kind for those who wrestle with its challenges.

Behind Robinson's teachings is a creation spirituality of the deepest kind, an invitation to commit to mysticism and carry that into the world of action or prophecy. A realization that the Godself (and Creation and Kingdom of God) are all of a part. We are already in heaven, the place where Divinity dwells. "Everything that is is holy" as the monk Thomas Merton wrote sixty years ago. Or as praise poet and creation mystic Mary Oliver put it in her poem "At the River Clarion," while sitting on a rock in the river, the water, the stone and the moss beneath the waters all told her, "I am part of holiness."[5]

All we need do is wake up to these facts and then let our behavior mirror that reality. To love as we are loved; to return grace for grace and blessing for blessing. To experience the Divine and create a culture that allows others to experience the Divine. What greater calling is there than this? John Robinson is to be praised for inviting us to so noble – and so necessary – a work.

Endnotes

1. Pierre Teilhard de Chardin, *Human Energy* (NY: Harcourt Brace Jovanovich, 1978), 82.

2. See Rupert Sheldrake, *Science Set Free* (NY: Random House, 2012), chapter on "Are Minds Confined to Brains?", 212-230.

3. Dorothee Soelle, *Theology for Skeptics: Reflections on God* (Minneapolis: Fortress Press, 1995), 50.

4. Ibid., 43f.

5. Mary Oliver, "At the River Clarion," in Mary Oliver, *Evidence: Poems by Mary Oliver* (Boston: Beacon Press, 2009), 51f. I cite the poem in its entirety in the chapter on the Cosmic Christ because it so richly names that archetype. See Matthew Fox, *Hildegard of Bingen: A Saint For Our Times* (Vancouver: Namaste Publishers, 2012), 18-22.

Preface

Finding, Losing and Recovering the Sacred Cosmos: A Personal Journey

I first witnessed Heaven on Earth as a child – a timeless, radiant, richly textured, sublime and sensuous reality permeated by an omnipresent loving consciousness. I had no words for this immersion in Creation but assumed everyone shared it. I experienced what William Wordsworth described,

> *There was a time when meadow, grove, and stream,*
> *The earth, and every common sight,*
> *To me did seem*
> *Apparelled in celestial light,*
> *The glory and the freshness of a dream.*

"Heaven," he said, "*lies about us in our infancy.*"

By age seven, I realized that adults no longer saw this lit world. Glassy-eyed stares and patronizing comments – "Isn't that sweet?" – diminished my enchantment. Soon I, too, doubted the magic and began to accept my required identity in the concept-driven World of Man, a patriarchal system of beliefs and values that drive "modern" civilization. I didn't want to be a concept but that seemed to be my only choice. My shining world was lost for decades. Wordsworth summed up this sad but universal sacrifice as well, acknowledging,

> *It is not now as it hath been of yore;-*
> *Turn wheresoe'er I may,*
> *By night or day,*
> *The things which I have seen I now can see no more...*
> *Shades of the prison-house begin to close*

Upon the growing boy...
At length the man perceives it die away,
And fade into the light of common day...

But I never forgot my sun-dappled world and, as I moved into middle age, my seeing grew brighter and I began to notice the divine world still existed all around me. At first, I dismissed this awakening vision. Perhaps I was crazy, I wondered, but as a clinical psychologist, I knew that wasn't true. I soon began exploring world religions like a madman searching for a lost treasure map and discovered that mystics from every tradition always corroborated what I saw – that Heaven on Earth is already here when we are awake enough to see it.

I continued studying the mystics with Matthew Fox, earning a second doctorate in Creation Spirituality in 2006, and at the Chaplaincy Institute, an interfaith seminary where I was ordained in 2008. Eventually I collected an amazing chorus of over a hundred mystic voices sharing my vision and published *Finding Heaven Here.* More importantly, I realized that the direct experience of Heaven on Earth holds the promise of a new way of life, a new kind of culture, and a remedy to the accelerating apocalypse of the human world. And, if we take it seriously, this vision also anticipates a new stage in humanity's spiritual evolution.

Heaven on Earth: Divine Humans in a Divine World

Heaven on Earth appears to us when the ordinary world is transfigured in the awakened experience of the divine, a perceptual realization universally found in firsthand accounts of mystical experience. This realized pantheism includes everything, even us – we are literally divine humans in a divine world and can learn to experience this revelation directly.

What happens as we step into the divine world? In the heightened consciousness of Heaven on Earth, people and things become incredibly beautiful, infinitely precious, and immanently holy. Our problems dissolve effortlessly in this always new and joyous consciousness. As the poet, William Blake, told us, "If the doors of perception were cleansed, everything would appear to man as it is, infinite."

Coming Home to the Sacred

Since early childhood, I have been following a single golden thread back to Heaven on Earth. Only now, in my seventies, do I understand the purpose of this journey. Rather than pursuing a particular theology or ministry, I was returning to a state of mystical consciousness that reveals all life to be sacred – not as a metaphor but as a lived and witnessed reality. This has been my calling through psychology, spirituality, and seminary; through nine books, countless talks and workshops; through personal psychotherapy, spiritual direction and mystical practices. It is the calling of the mystic to the sacred.

Aging became another part of this calling. I was ordained not to a new career but to a time of life with unique consciousness and tasks – and to me, this meant living in the mystical consciousness of Heaven on Earth and sharing it with a world in trouble. I move now in a new state of consciousness in which everything I do is part of my calling and every action I take is sacred action in the service of a sacred world. Awakened aging has been a baptism sanctifying my life and my new role as spiritual elder. If ordination represents a sacred covenant with divinity and religious community, then this was mine, and I stepped across its threshold.

Why I Wrote This Book

I had concluded in recent years that my writing life was finished, that I had said all I came here to say. I focused instead on my own spiritual growth and awakening the gifts I might still share in these troubled times. Often deep in mystical consciousness,

I recorded ongoing experiences of awakening as they came, typing them single spaced for over two hundred pages. I simply called it *Revelations*. Then one day, I felt compelled to write again, to apply my previous work and these new realizations to the apocalyptic time now descending upon all of us.

This book weaves together 25 years of mystical writing with new insights from a single unfolding revelation, one that has taken me a lifetime to understand, and it invites you, the reader, to experience this revelation as well. If you take this material seriously, if you explore its lessons and experiential exercises with sincerity, your consciousness will transform and an entirely new way of being in the world will be awakened. As you embrace the experience of being a divine human in a divine world, you will understand how civilization has failed and what it will take to return humanity to its ultimate spiritual potential. Mysticism begins as an individual encounter with the divine. We can transform the world but we must start with our own transformation. I wrote this book to awaken your inborn potential as a mystical activist. Help us save Creation.

Introduction

Mysticism: A Deep Way of Knowing, A New Kind of Seeing

Mystical Activism: Transforming a World in Crisis takes us from our universal experience of Heaven on Earth in childhood to the awakening of human civilization. It is an invitation to transform your personality, life, work, spirituality, religion, even the world itself, to become a divine human in a divine world, and a mystical activist in a time of apocalyptic cultural, political and climate disruption.

To call these "end times" is hardly hyperbolic. We are in trouble and the signs are everywhere: extreme political divisions; xenophobic violence; wealth inequity; poverty and homelessness; persistent racism, sexism, and ageism; cruelty toward indigenous peoples; arms buildups and unending wars; and, most threatening of all, terrifying climate disruption. Associated with man-made global warming, climate change is already resulting in food and water shortages, species extinctions, unlivable climate zones, and catastrophic weather, flood and fire events. It is also obvious that we are the cause of these dark times. Each of these crises originates in the human psyche – yours and mine. Driven by left-brain beliefs, illusions, addictions and obsessions, we race headlong toward the collapse of civilization. Fortunately, the solution to these mounting crises also lies in the human psyche, arising from a most surprising source: the right-brain's natural mystical consciousness. Our survival depends on whether we understand and resolve this paradox in time.

The crisis before us demands not only social, political and technological action but also a mystically-infused metamorphosis of personality, relationships, and our perception of the entire

11

Earth community. We need not abandon science, social activism, technology or interfaith dialogue, but we must add mystical consciousness to our local and global activism. Merging right-brain mystical awareness with left-brain science and logic, we integrate the mystic's consciousness into our urgent collective mobilization.

The Mystic's Great Vision

Whenever humanity teeters on a terrifying cliff edge, mystics offer hope and it always begins with our own personal transformation. The essence of this vision can be summarized in five universal mystical realizations and their potential for a new world:

1. The cosmos is conscious, awake, aware, welcoming, and constantly unfolding as Creation itself, infusing everything with an infinitely loving omnipresence and reaffirming humanity's original pantheism. The Earth is literally divine, arising from the very substance, nature and being of God. We live in an infinitely holy place filled with sacred beings, human and otherwise.

2. Human beings, driven by left-brain thinking, create and project an illusory world over our divine home, a mental world ugly with stereotypical beliefs, invented conflicts, endless problems, and nonstop fantasy, but we can, just as easily, erase these illusions in the sensory clarity of mystical consciousness.

3. How do we transform the world? It begins and ends with this realization: All consciousness is divine consciousness. Dissolving the ego's perpetual fascination with its false self and imaginary world, we unmask our own divinity and awaken a life divine. Dwelling in

divine consciousness transforms our experience of self, our work and the world itself.

4. When we fully appreciate who and where we really are – divine beings in a divine world – we will cease harming our sacred planet and our imaginary problems will fade away as, when a movie ends, the lights come on, and we realize we've all been in a collective trance. This awakening creates a new kind of activism – mystical activism – based on literally witnessing the sacredness of life on Earth.

5. As our individual and collective transformation proceed, we won't abandon the world of planes, trains, computers and corporations central to modern life; rather we will transform them with the love and mystical intelligence inherent in the divine mind.

I am not asking you to *believe* this revelation, but I am confident that you will *experience* it if you try. With my heart and soul, I beseech you to try. Humanity's renewal is less a matter of faith than of transformed vision. Just as the divine world is never finished, neither is mystical revelation – we will be divinely guided through the death and rebirth of civilization if we pay attention. As the mind clears, so too does the path, and this unfolding vision will be further developed and affirmed as we progress through each chapter.

This apocalyptic time in history represents a profound evolutionary challenge urgently calling us to the next level of spiritual awakening. We are all mystics seeking a new revelation for the world. Happily, this mystical shift begins in the joy of personal transformation. Thereafter, wisdom to heal the world flows directly from the divine into personal mystical consciousness and being. It is direct illumination that we seek, not political or theological debate. If we awaken the firsthand experience of divinity, life will flourish; if we fail to awaken it, we will surely suffer or perish from our own stubbornness and egocentric stupidity. Those who pursue the path of enlightenment will learn to dream a new dream of humanity, replacing the illusions of identity, time and story with the creative power of love, beauty and enchantment. We will enter the mind of God to welcome unprecedented new insights and resources for our journey, and we will become divine humans in the process.

Preparing to Read This Book

Before we start, I want to reflect on the topic of mysticism itself. What goes through your mind hearing the word *mysticism*? Are you excited and fascinated in anticipation of what you may discover, or skeptical, doubtful, maybe even a little uncomfortable?

The reason I bring this up is that the mystical consciousness we'll be exploring – and you will experience – can be instantly short-circuited by a single skeptical or critical thought. Because mysticism has endured centuries of condemnation, ridicule, disbelief and persecution from Western religion, I would expect some degree of skepticism from even the most open-minded. Can you imagine how your childhood priest, minister, pastor, or rabbi would have responded if you, echoing Hildegard, proclaimed, "I am the fiery life of God!" Would you have encountered an expression of joy and approval, or disapproval and correction? Negative memories, conscious and unconscious, can automatically trigger old doubts and fears of criticism.

Western religion's historical disapproval of mysticism stems from the mystics' direct experience of divinity. Firsthand revelation undermines the power of religious authority, rendering mystics as perceived threats to institutional religion. It doesn't have to be this way, of course, for all religions are birthed from mystical experiences, but not infrequently clerics emphasize belief and conformity over direct experience.

And science has been no more helpful. I grew up in a family with no formal religion. Or put differently, our religions were science and psychoanalysis. When I asked my father, a scientist, about religion as a boy, he said, "Oh, John! You don't need religion. Natural scientific explanations can account for what we see." On his deathbed, however, he confided, "Don't be sad. I have seen the other side. I am not afraid to die." Deathbed visions had made him a mystic.

And what about psychology? My mother was a Freudian when I was little and, as you know, Freud dismissed religion and mysticism as neuroses. This subtle psychological prejudice continues among many psychotherapists today. But on her deathbed, dying from dementia, my mother was talking to people we couldn't see asking them, "Well, what am I going to do when I get there?" She was a social activist always looking for good works. I guess they continue in the next world.

What about society? If you say, "I am a divine being," to your neighbor, in the grocery store, or at the airport, most people will respond with shock, disbelief or ridicule, or suggest time in a psychiatric hospital. I'm a clinical psychologist with a second doctorate in ministry – I know the difference between psychiatric patients and mystics, a difference well supported by the literature. Psychiatric patients who say these kinds of things are delusional, tormented by frightening or demeaning beliefs and hallucinations, and profoundly alienated from others. Mystics, on the other hand, are loving, caring, and relational; they often see the world differently from mystical consciousness and are imbued with joy, gratitude, and deep spiritual insight. While some mystics evolve into prophets who can be fierce and confrontational in the face of injustice, they are not crazy. In fact, the research also suggests that they may be mentally healthier than the average person.

I bring all this up because I want you to *experience* this book, not unconsciously discount it with old conditioned skepticism, fixed opinions, religious guilt, or fear of disapproval. I am probably preaching to the choir here, but even the choir is part of a collective mindset that minimizes the power and significance of the mystical experience. You picked up this book for a reason. I would bet mystical consciousness is part of that reason. Don't lose your golden thread.

Ready, Set, Go!

Mystical Activism: Transforming a World in Crisis combines original material from earlier books with inspiring new insights, perspectives and tools to address today's political, social and environmental destabilization. If you discover a theme you wish to explore further, read the book associated with that theme listed in the Appendix. We will also be plowing new territory, revealing the unprecedented power of mystical consciousness to heal humanity's terrible divisions. Mystical activism is neither trivial nor imaginary. I believe that our personal and collective salvation now depends on reawakening humanity's mystical potential, a realization that has never been so clear to me, or clearly articulated, in the modern era.

As you can see from the Contents, *Part I, Understanding Our Apocalyptic Age* explains what has gone wrong in the world and the role spirituality can play in beginning the transformational journey of healing, followed by discussions of the nature and power of mystical experience, its relationship to Presence, and how the religious psyche contributes to both causing and solving our problems. After building this foundation, *Part II, Mystical Transformation* awakens your natural mystical ability, opening a perception of the divine world – where it is, why you don't see it, and how you can – and yourself as a divine human – who you really are. We then explore the transformational possibilities, conscious sacred aging and the timeless mystical insights revealed in myth and fairy tale. In *Part III, Mystical*

Activism, we apply our newly awakened mystical consciousness to the problems of the world, present a revolutionary new understanding of soul, discover help from the "other side," and guide you to the unique gifts you came here to give the world. After confronting the decline of the aging patriarchy, we end with a discussion of the ultimate power of mystical activism in transforming a world in crisis.

All along this path you will find *experiential exercises* for transforming yourself and bringing the mystical consciousness into your own life and work. These are powerful workshop-tested exercises for experiencing mystical awareness, Heaven on Earth, and the amazing potential of mystical dialogues for meeting soul, divinity, ancestors and other spiritual beings. Like learning to swim from reading a book, you will not fully understand mystical consciousness until you experience it firsthand; then all I say will make the most amazing sense. Go slowly through the exercises, one step at a time, letting the experience unfold before moving on, and understand that this is an evolving process. If you've had no experience with meditation or mindfulness, you might be frustrated at first but that will change. Also, if the instructions involve closing your eyes, you might record them for yourself.

Finally, this book contains many exciting ideas about mysticism and how it can be applied to the crises of this apocalyptic time. As you read, you may want to underline, page mark, take notes, or otherwise keep track of the ideas that stir you, for they represent the stepping-stones of your own unique path through this challenging time. This is a workbook on your own transformation and a revelation of the gifts only you can bring to our struggling world.

Part I

Understanding Our Apocalyptic Age: The Dominance of the False Self in a False World

Chapter 1

What's Happening to Our World? A Modern Creation Story

Anyone paying attention to the news knows we are in trouble. The red warning lights now flashing in scientific reports, changing Earth conditions and political extremism have been signaling an accelerating disequilibrium for some time, heralding coastal flooding, heat waves, droughts, storms, water wars, fascist governments, mass migrations, species extinctions, epidemics, insect infestations, on and on.

The question posed above – "What's happening to our world?" – can be approached with scientific, political, and historical analyses. This book examines this impending train wreck from yet another vantage point – an ancient and symbolic one – the power of myth. Not an old myth this time, that will come later, but a new one, one I wrote a decade ago as I sensed humanity's escalating crisis. Myths ascend from the archetypal depths of human psyche, as this one came to me, and I believe that you will find it as powerful as I did.

This modern creation story symbolically depicts humanity's rise and fall. Not unlike the long Biblical journey from Genesis to Revelations, or indeed countless other creation stories, it moves from worship and wonder to grandiosity and disaster, for the deep psyche seems to understand that Creation is not a one-time affair, but an evolving one, and always accompanied by the same fatal human flaw – our betrayal of the sacred ground of existence. Born of divinity, as the universal story goes, humans live in harmony with creation for a time, but sooner or later, overtaken by the self-centered reflections of Narcissus in the reflection pool, we abandon the divine world for another one, a world created by and for the ego. We now live in that world.

This archetypal theme of original wonder and subsequent forgetting describes our long evolutionary journey now reaching another inevitable and tragic tipping point. But this time around, the risks are catastrophically high – global war, unlivable landscapes, starvations, and the breakdown of civilization. This crisis tops all others and, unchecked, will be devastating for future generations. We urgently need to wake up, for the answers can only come through us.

This book is about the psyche, yours and mine, for humanity's epic struggle arises from the psyche's universal archetypal structure that both generates and dissolves our problems. We will work with a new model of the psyche to understand our part in this crisis and discover humanity's inborn mystical response that restores the divine world to save humanity from itself. Called *Heaven's Compass*, the model is implicit in this modern creation story, symbolically revealing what's gone wrong and how we can re-awaken our perception of the mystical ground of Creation once again. Most importantly, this story describes *our* psyche and the journey we must take to discover the divine in ourselves and the world.

A Modern Creation Story

In the beginning, only Divinity existed as a realm unto itself: pure consciousness and potentiality. Wishing to know itself in a new way, the divine burst forth in a fiery expansion of light and matter evolving the entire cosmos from its own essence. The divine became the universe and, in an act of infinite love and generosity, gave birth to a holy place called Earth. Divinity suffused everything with its own unique and unfolding nature – sea, rocks, plants, animals, weather, seasons. Thus, Creation became a second divine realm – the physical world as a manifestation of divinity.

Among all the creatures that evolved from Creation, one developed the unique capacity to think abstractly, to form concepts about the world and even to reflect on its own existence and relationship to the sacred. This creature was a part of divinity becoming conscious of itself and of the universe in a new way – a wondrous epiphany. Thus, the human species came into being. In time, the human capacity for thought produced many marvelous inventions, including religion, agriculture, literature, architecture, science, engineering, medicine, and technology – a divinely inspired explosion of human creativity.

At the same time, however, something strange began to happen – human beings became so fascinated with their concepts about the world that they began to mistake their concepts for the world itself. In other words, people increasingly saw only what they thought. Soon names, ideas, beliefs, and stories constructed a third and separate mental realm – the World of Man, and the sacred ground of Creation gradually disappeared from human consciousness. Worse, entranced by the power of concepts, people began to view the natural world as simply a source of wealth or raw materials, a place to be conquered, controlled, used, and discarded. They stopped listening to the voices of Creation – such as the disappearing species, the shattered ecosystems and the displaced indigenous peoples – that spoke instead of damage, degradation and suffering.

Now at the center of humankind's third realm was the idea of self, a concept that became both a blessing and a curse. On the positive side, the self-concept allowed individuals to look within and discover much about their psychological, spiritual and mystical nature. On the negative side, however, the self-concept simply became too important. Humans became obsessed with this idea and soon everyone worried about the worth, goodness, beauty, power, wealth, immortality and importance of the personal self. Tragically, this self-centeredness spawned ever-increasing competition, conflict and even warfare.

Living in the complicated World of Man, people betrayed and then forgot their divine nature and homeland, and this betrayal and forgetting created a fourth and final realm: Darkness. It became a murky hidden space filled with the pain, anger and grief accumulated by each new generation of children coerced to deny their natural divinity and believe instead that only the World of Man mattered.

Those who struggled with their inner Darkness usually believed it was a sign of weakness and tried to overcome it by constantly improving their self-concept, or, if that failed, by finding ways to medicate the hurt into numbness. Some even imagined this Darkness to be far away in a horrible underworld called Hell. In either case, few wanted to visit this seemingly grim and gloomy landscape, not realizing that it was the World of Man, not Darkness, that had become grim and gloomy. Their tragic lack of understanding about this realm caused them to miss its precious gifts and opportunities, for an amazing source of healing and creativity now lay hidden in Darkness.

With diminishing joy, people in the World of Man concluded that they had been expelled from Creation. Some viewed this expulsion as divine punishment for their pursuit of knowledge, no longer remembering that humans had lost interest in the direct perception of Creation in the first place. Entranced by the power of the intellect and the grandiosity of the ego, they had forgotten how to see the divine realm. Because they no longer witnessed or believed in Creation here on Earth, people erroneously imagined that both the Creator and the sacred world had relocated somewhere else, far away, in a place they called Heaven. That realm, they assumed, only existed beyond this physical life.

Seduced by the imagined possibilities of self-importance, people decided that by acquiring enough wealth, power, fame, or perfection they still could find a substitute Heaven on Earth. As the World of Man grew ever more powerful, so did the forces of selfishness, greed, narcissism, and grandiosity. The Earth began dying from humanity's abuse and exploitation.

As time went on, people occasionally would catch glimpses of the original world — for after all, Creation had never left and seeing it was still possible — but most, enmeshed in the World of Man, disbelieved their eyes and hurried on to the next problem, self-improvement project or grand activity. A few rare individuals, however, stopped to look more closely and realized that Heaven existed not just in the future but here, now, on Earth as well. More importantly, they discovered that whenever they sensed Divinity's presence here, Heaven on Earth appeared all around them – in their gardens, families, and communities; Heaven was just another name for Creation. Some of these people became great mystics, prophets, or social activists. Others just lived in simple happiness or service. In either case, for these few the World of Man and its underlying Darkness had become transparent, allowing them to see the radiance of the divine shining through everything.

Sadly, the vast majority of people in the World of Man still failed to see Heaven on Earth and continued under the spell of destructive and erroneous beliefs, rationalizing, "It's a dog eat dog world," "Suck it up!" or "Wealth equals worth." As a consequence, the assault on nature and wars between peoples continued, bringing the human species to the edge of extinction. The most desperate believed that only the apocalyptic end of the world would bring Heaven on Earth. Few understood that the future of humankind depended on all people finding and sharing Heaven on Earth right here, right now.

Chapter 2

Spirituality: A Good Place to Begin

Most of us hold spiritual beliefs of some sort, clear or vague, agnostic or devout, and it can be fascinating to share them – if we can do so respectfully! Our spiritual beliefs can also be a challenge to summarize. Have you ever tried to list your basic beliefs in three sentences? It's a good exercise for achieving a spiritual perspective on yourself but it raises some important questions.

What is Spirituality?

Is spirituality about living in the moment, feeling one with God, asking profound questions, sensing the inner divine, cultivating faith and devotion, discovering inner peace, serving others, following religious commandments, coping with pain and grief, seeking the meaning of life, surrendering to the flow, pursuing a just world, confirming the essential truths of religion, confronting suffering and evil, transcending the ego, spreading God's love, receiving guidance from angels or spirit guides, learning meditation, understanding Near-Death or Out-of-Body Experiences, or finding the sacred in everyday life? These are but a handful of the innumerable ways people describe their spirituality.

How can we make sense of all this diversity? Here's the answer. Spirituality refers to the *individual meaning* we create about life from our religious education, everyday experiences and moments of sacred connection. In other words, our spirituality represents the personal conclusions we've reached so far about the nature and purpose of life, divinity, and the universe. Given the breadth of human experience and the diversity of personality styles, it's not surprising so many different interpretations of religious theology and scripture exist – there are as many answers as people. This fact also explains how spirituality differs from religion. For example, a congregation of 300 members will have one formal religion but 300 unique spiritual interpretations of that religion. In other words, we find the truths closest to our own heart and life circumstances.

Spirituality is part of humankind's universal religious search. We sense a divine reality or principle within or behind the material world and endeavor to grasp its purpose and function in our lives. We also tend to believe that the pain and confusion of life, and indeed all that befalls us, is somehow related to this divine order, and when we are in trouble, atheist and believer alike, often cry out one of God's many names. And, as we will discover, in the depths of the human personality lies the religious psyche, a numinous center that is itself divine and whispers its secret counsel in that "still small voice within." In this way, spirituality also serves as a stepping-stone from formal religion, with its history, scriptures, theology and practices, to firsthand mystical experiences of the divine where we encounter the revelations of religion for ourselves.

What is Spirituality For?

If there are so many different meanings to spirituality, what is its purpose? What is it really for? Again, many answers come to mind. Spirituality is about...

Searching for Ultimate Understanding. Humans are natural philosophers and theologians. Sooner or later, we ponder the ultimate questions of existence, such as "Why am I here?" "What is the purpose of life?" "Does God exist?" "What is the nature of sin, suffering and evil?" "How should we live our lives?" "Can we know the divine directly?" and "What happens when we die?" While religions may formally address these questions, coming to terms with them for ourselves is central to personal spiritual growth and understanding.

Deepening Our Connection with the Divine. Religion and spirituality provide ways of reaching out to the divine, including worship, prayer, contemplation, meditation, ritual, fasting, art and dance. Going deeply into a spiritual practice can provide a real and felt connection to the divine, including firsthand mystical awareness, allowing us to experience religious truths for ourselves and deepen our relationship with the sacred.

Coping Positively with Stress, Trauma and Loss. Spiritual beliefs can be a positive source for coping with stress, trauma and loss. When terrible things happen, we ask profound and sincere questions about the significance of the event that go beyond physical facts to the level of transcendent meaning and causation. "Why did God take my wife?" "Why did this accident have to happen to me?" "Why is my friend suffering so much?" Our spiritual beliefs, readings, prayers and practices stir both answers and comfort, helping us bear the unbearable, find new meaning in our struggle, and provide hope for the future.

Growing Our Experience of the Divine. The spiritual journey moves through many stages over our lifetime. The young child's natural intuitions of divinity, simple, imaginative and unexamined, are eventually overwritten with more conceptual explanations from adults, first in the form of stories and then formal beliefs. As adolescents, we may question these stories and beliefs with logic and facts but eventually form our own evolving theology as we move through life. As we age, an intuitive experiential understanding of the divine often grows inside, reenergizing the spiritual journey. Looking back on our lives, we see and value this process of spiritual maturation that not only brings wisdom but may also prepare us for death.

Discovering Aging as a New Spiritual Stage. Our new and unprecedented longevity now initiates people into a new stage of spiritual life, potentially transforming our experience of self, consciousness and reality. Pursuing the amazing possibilities of this new time, we discover opportunities for spiritual growth, service and sacred activism that can change the world. Older people are not problems, they are resources, wisdom keepers, family historians, holders of tradition, artists, mentors, and aging examples for the young.

Recognizing What Spirituality Is Not For. Our understanding of spirituality would be incomplete without recognizing the cost of negative beliefs. Considerable psychological research confirms the very real harm caused by beliefs that make us feel unworthy, ashamed, powerless, guilty or afraid. We are not "sinners in the hands of an angry God" doomed to eternal damnation, and using religious and spiritual authority, beliefs or quotations to manipulate, control, judge or threaten others is never healthy or constructive.

Final Things to Consider...

- Keep searching for what feels personally real and valid in your own spiritual journey – it is your journey.
- Turn to spiritual intuitions, readings, and religions in times of pain and struggle and let them reveal personal truths you may already know but haven't fully appreciated.
- Remember that spirituality often moves from beliefs to direct experiences as we grow and age, so pursue the journey into firsthand awareness of the divine as well.
- Avoid beliefs or practitioners that cause you to feel fear, pain, helplessness, inferiority, confusion, shame or guilt.
- Know that you are inherently beautiful, precious and unconditionally loved.

Spirituality is also intended to crack open the door to the next stage of the divine journey: firsthand mystical experience.

Chapter 3

Mysticism: Where Visionary Transformation Originates

Mystical awakening represents one of the most important experiences in human life, bringing profound religious understanding, forming or confirming our deepest values, and changing our very nature as human beings. As described earlier, mysticism was disparaged, distrusted and suppressed for centuries. In disguised form, it came roaring back in the 1960s when the young, tired of uninspired religious services, began experimenting with Eastern religious practices, psychedelic drugs and the "spiritual not religious" identity searching anew for authentic mystical experience. As we will see, this timeless human search for ultimate, life-transforming vision and realization always leads back to the same amazing experience.

What is Mysticism?

Briefly, mysticism refers to the direct, firsthand experience of the divine. People have been having mystical experiences since the dawn of time, from major figures like Jesus, Buddha, Moses, and Mohammad, whose revelations evolved into world religions, to everyday folks like you and me touched by the power and profundity of these sacred moments.

In general, mystical experiences come in three flavors: big mystical experiences, little mystical experiences and mystical consciousness.

Big mystical experiences, known variously as enlightenment, satori, cosmic consciousness, peak experiences, and countless other names, transform an individual's life with their power and profundity. You rarely forget a big mystical experience. In fact, its sacred energy and realizations are often rekindled, re-

31

experienced and expanded when we share them.

Little mystical experiences arise in states of awe and reverence evoked by great natural beauty, powerful rituals, or profound moments of life. Examples include the stunning miracle of childbirth, the spectacle of Midnight Mass, the magic of falling in love, an awestruck moment witnessing natural beauty, or the sacred transition of death. These are potentially times when the mind momentarily stops its incessant chatter, perception heightens, and you sense something sacred right before your eyes. We've all had little mystical experiences though we may have overlooked, misinterpreted or forgotten their spiritual significance.

Finally, mystical consciousness is a way of intentionally awakening the direct perception of the divine in order to explore the same qualities and dimensions of big and little mystical experiences though often with less intensity. While people have long believed that mystical experiences are beyond our control, over the years it has become clear to me that we also have the ability to perceive divinity directly. This mystical awareness can be achieved with various spiritual practices and exercises – we'll be exploring many in later chapters – and offers us an amazing laboratory for direct experience of our divine self and world.

In sum, we have big mystical experiences, little mystical experiences, and mystical consciousness. The big mystical experiences happen spontaneously, breakthroughs of the divine that are beyond our control, the little ones are triggered by what's happening around us, and mystical consciousness can be intentionally evoked, teaching us a great deal about the divine and transforming us in the process. Moreover, all these mystical states involve the same experience of a sacred, timeless, loving Presence whose consciousness permeates the universe and blesses us with...

- Transfiguring perceptions of reality as luminous, sacred,

and infinitely precious

- Reassurance of Creation's perfection, holiness and purpose
- A personal experience of immense unconditional love
- Feelings of gratitude and humility for the gift of life
- Personal revelations of insight, meaning, or other sacred teachings.

Personal Examples

Have you ever had a big or little mystical experience? They are far more common than we realize. Abraham Maslow, the father of humanistic psychology, called them "peak experiences" and discovered that nearly everyone could identify personal examples when asked the right questions. Let me give you some examples of big mystical experiences to stir your memory. Read them slowly. Try to sense for yourself what's happening. This man recalled...

The room in which I was standing looked out onto the backyards of a tenement. The buildings were decrepit and ugly, the ground covered with boards, rags, and debris. Suddenly every object in my field of vision took on a curious and intense kind of existence of its own... And every object, seen under this aspect, appeared exceedingly beautiful. There was a cat out there with its head lifted, effortlessly watching a wasp that moved without moving just above its head. Everything was urgent with life... which was the same in the cat, the wasp, and the broken bottles, and merely manifested itself differently in these individuals... All things seemed to glow with a light that came from within them... I experienced a complete certainty that at that moment I saw things as they really were, and I was filled with grief at the realization of the real situation of human beings, living continuously in the midst of all this without being aware of it... I saw how absurd had been my expectations of a vision of God... For I had no doubt that I had seen God; that is, had seen all there is to see. Yet it turned out to be the world that I looked at every day.

Here's another example. Walking home from the train station, this person recalled,

It was now that I found myself looking at a certain house, one with which I am very familiar, as if I had never seen it before... According to one's ordinary perceptions, it is rather an ugly little suburban villa; but now it appeared to be quite otherwise... I stood and stared at it, and the mere sight of it filled me with an indescribable joy... I realized that, could one always live on this level then the whole world would be changed; it would be another world in which there would be nothing which we habitually call ugly or evil... everything I saw was mysterious and wonderful... My ability to see, my actual and physical eyesight, was greatly sharpened... the sheer joy I experienced in all this is beyond expression. I felt that the world of nature was utterly right and literally an act of God's, and that to know this, and to be permitted to appreciate so much of the wonderful and the adorable, was nothing less than bliss. And this was reality. That is the whole point. The feelings and thoughts we usually have are not real by comparison with this new condition of being into which I had moved... At one point in this walk, it flashed upon me with the same effect of irrefutable conviction: Of course there is a God... God was here; he was in everything I looked at and in me who looked... I was in God's presence.

And one more...

Often during my late twenties and early thirties I had a good deal of depression... at the age of thirty-three, I felt I must be going mad. I felt shut up in a cocoon in complete isolation and could not get in touch with anyone... things came to such a pass and I was so tired of fighting that I said one day, "I can do no more. Let nature, or whatever is behind the universe, look after me now." ...

Within a few days I passed from hell to a heaven. It was as if the cocoon had burst and my eyes were opened and I saw... The world was infinitely beautiful, full of light as if from an inner radiance. Everything was alive and God was present in all things; in fact, the earth, all plants and animals and people seemed to be made of God. All things were one, and I was one with all creation and held safe within a deep love. I was filled with peace and joy and with deep humility, and could only bow down in the holiness of the presence of God... It was as if scales had fallen from my eyes and I saw the world as it truly was.

Do these descriptions remind you of a small or big mystical experience from your own life? The more we listen to others' mystical experiences, the more we discover our own.

What, then, is the ultimate meaning of these mystical experiences? The profound and startling answer is this: The universe and everything in it is literally alive as one conscious, loving and divine being, including us. Experiencing this consciousness creates the conviction that the immediate, love-drenched *now* is the goal of existence. Awakened from our customary slumber in the mental world of identity, time and story, with its endless self-generated problems and conflicts, we discover that everything is already sacred, even us. If we could learn to live in this awakened state, our lives would be forever changed. This experience offers us the means and the goal of mystical activism.

Experiencing Mystical Consciousness

The obvious next step in our journey is the actual experience of mystical consciousness. Mystical consciousness is an intentional state of intense, highly sensory awareness that dissolves the veil of thought to reveal the presence of the divine as reality itself. The shift into mystical consciousness has four steps. Though the steps are remarkably simple, the art is to fully *experience* each step. The more you experience, the deeper you go.

Before we move into the experience of mystical consciousness, let's get familiar with its nature and then reflect on when you may have spontaneously experienced these steps. Here are the keys that unlock awakened consciousness.

Keys to Mystical Consciousness

1. *Stop Thinking.* Because we tend to see only what we think, not what is right before us, quieting the mind is important. Despite what people often say, it's not hard to stop thinking, at least for short periods. For example, when we're focusing sensory perception in a fine-motor task, like threading a needle or painting trim, the mind stops its chatter. We can't think about our taxes or a recent family upset without missing the hole or dripping the paint. This kind of sensory focus developed naturally in our evolution as a survival skill – when our ancestors heard a lion growl nearby, thinking automatically stopped! It happens naturally when we shift into the pure sensory perception.

2. *Heighten Awareness.* In this step, we awaken ourselves as much as possible. We all know how to do this, as when the morning alarm fails to go off and we are suddenly late for work! We tell ourselves, "Wake Up!" and we move from sleepy to speedy in seconds.

3. *Experience the World Exactly as It Is.* In this step, we focus this pure and intense sensory perception on things around us and, adding a little awe, begin to witness the extraordinary beauty of Creation. Beauty is always here when you really look! And, because we are looking directly into God's conscious being, this step further

awakens mystical consciousness.

4. *Come into the Presence.* Finally, we learn to experience the divine Presence which further sanctifies perception. We experience the Presence through spiritual practices or visiting holy places. It can also be found in pure consciousness, for the mystics tell us that all consciousness is divine consciousness. To be conscious of consciousness, therefore, is to experience God directly.

One of the wonderful things we learn from this practice is the extraordinary beauty and freshness of everyday life. It heals us naturally, because thought-free sensory consciousness is where the divine is found, where wisdom arises naturally, and where our hearts live. It is a taste of Heaven on Earth! In the presence of loved ones, dancing in the kitchen to the smell of minestrone, and bath time for a two-year-old, we find divinity spontaneously expressed in life's immediate moments and details, especially when we cease thinking. We pay full attention and find wonder. God is in the little things when we're not looking for God.

We will experience these keys through numerous experiential practices in upcoming chapters, taking us ever more deeply into the divine fabric of our lives. In anticipation of this experience, I'd like to whet your appetite by sharing my own experience of mystical consciousness, one that always transfigures my perception of self, reality and divinity.

When I move into mystical consciousness, I enter an awakened state – calm, holy, grateful, relieved and loving. Everything feels different now. Time is timeless. All is flow. Identity has vanished and I am ageless. I feel deep relief from the burden of being someone. I move more slowly, consciously, staying in the present. The world is magical, amazing, radiant, alive, colorful, light-filled, enchanting, beautiful and mysterious. It calls me ever deeper into communion with its living presence. And I am as mysterious, amazing and beautiful as everything else. I feel the consciousness of divinity infusing "me" with its energy, and transforming my being and perception. I return to Heaven on Earth. Everything I touch and see now is divine, alive with divinity's "is-ness," vibrant, animated and bursting with love. So much love. No longer a prisoner of identity or belief, I am one with everything, and the experience keeps intensifying and expanding. I am centered in the divine as the divine. Everywhere I go, my awakened state says, "I love you," and envelops the world in joy. The all-pervading "rightness" of this consciousness allows me to accept whatever is happening around me without interpretation, judgment or reactivity, for thinking would cloud my awareness with irrelevant ideas and beliefs and shut off my love. As I stay in this highly sensory mode, I am no longer the "doer" but doing happens, and I contribute effortlessly to Creation by simply being love and surrendering to the immense and timeless flow of its goodness.

I appreciate that this description will either seem altogether perfect or completely crazy depending on your own experience with mystical states. Whatever the case, stay curious and try to avoid judgments, for we are entering a consciousness that transcends thought. Sooner or later we have to choose between analysis and awakening, between the World of Man and Heaven on Earth.

A New Understanding of God

One more consideration as we prepare for our mystical journey. For eons, humans have viewed God as a huge, external, and all-knowing human-like figure who rewards some, punishes others, and ignores many, and whose actions in the world often seem mysterious and inexplicable. This is the projection model of God. We created this figure of God in our own image and still project this figure "out there" somewhere! Worse, this belief assigns the responsibility for change onto a fictional character to whom we pray hoping that he, she, or it will someday hear us, or do what we ask, or show us why things are the way they are, or something!

The mystics tell us, however, that the cosmos is completely saturated and infused with divine consciousness, including us. They say the divine is closer than our own breath, nearer than thought, always present, and ultimately our truest self. In other words, we are literally made of God for the divine is everything. If you want to know divinity, they say, know yourself.

Experiencing the mystical unity of self and Self allows us to move from a *dualistic* relationship with the divine – you and divinity – to a *nondual* experience – you as divinity, divinity as you. Then, it's not about praying to a particular divine figure, it's about dissolving into the divine and experiencing its consciousness as our own. While both dual and nondual mystical experience are legitimate ways of knowing and serving the divine, the latter allows us to be lived by divinity. Indeed, I believe the next stage of humanity's spiritual evolution will come from the intentional awaking of the divine Self in each of us. If this is true, then we are the problem, for we refuse to accept our transformation into God.

Finally, many people have difficulty with the word "God." They correctly say that this word has too much negative baggage for them and for the culture. While finding a better word for God can help, it's difficult to find a name everyone can agree on, and the real challenge is to face our own personal wounding related to that word. We won't fix our wounds with a different word, because the wound will still be there. Instead, we need to find and tell the story of our wounding, work it through, release its pain, and wake up to who and where we really are. If a word disrupts our equanimity, then we are prisoners of that word and of a trauma that will continue to arrest our spiritual growth until we transcend it.

Religion, Spirituality and Mysticism

The difference between religion and spirituality was previously discussed, but there is one more important distinction. Mysticism is not about beliefs, it's about perception – the direct and transformational perception of ultimate reality. Although it may lead to or confirm religious or spiritual beliefs, mystical experience itself requires neither and can occur in the absence of belief or to those with atheist convictions. In this way, mysticism is in a category by itself, free from any particular dogma or theology, making it available and useful to activists across the religious and nonreligious spectrum.

Mystical experience is the heart and soul of mystical activism. It is the key to transforming self and world, and the power we each possess to change humanity's course in this apocalyptic time.

Chapter 4

Heaven's Compass: Introducing the Split-Brain

How does our psyche produce the very problems we are trying to solve, and how might it solve these problems instead? Our modern creation story described four states of consciousness that contribute both to our current global crisis and, potentially, to its solution. We turn now to the model revealed in this story to explore its lessons for our own lives and the approaching apocalypse.

The spiritual journey – its problems and its joys – originates from four states of consciousness. Each state is, in effect, a "land" of our psycho-spiritual nature through which we travel on our long journey home to the sacred. As we unfold the map of our collective adventures in consciousness, reflect on how your life fits its winding course. While the model may seem complicated at first, it is actually quite simple and you will soon find yourself using it to understand your feelings, struggles, and divinely-revealed next steps.

The Split Psyche

Many millennia ago, as humans were evolving their remarkable speech, language and conceptual abilities, a curious thing happened. The cerebral cortex began structuring two separate – though highly interconnected – states of consciousness. The left hemisphere specialized in the language skills critical for survival. Now humans could define social roles, pass on discoveries from previous generations, record their history, create science and technology, make long-range plans, and tell stories about their lives. This process also created the ego that soon took charge of the personality and became director of consciousness. While this conceptual programming of the left-brain was unfolding, the right-brain maintained its already highly developed capacities for here-and-now awareness, visual-spatial analysis, emotional intelligence, and facial recognition. It also maintained its mystical consciousness – the awakened thought-free sensory consciousness of the sacred present.

Sadly, as time passed, our right-brain mystical consciousness was progressively demoted – thought and speech seemed far more exciting to the ego. Without direct access to speech and language functions, the right-brain could no longer compete with the ego for director of consciousness or spokesperson for reality. Little by little, language replaced mystical perception, we stopped seeing Creation, and humanity came to dwell entirely in its own labyrinthine construction – the World of Man. Worse, the evolution of split-brain consciousness left a terrible nostalgia in the psyche. We unconsciously miss Creation. We grieve for it. We seek it in all kinds of substitutes. And, knowing that we now stand at the edge of a terrible precipice, we must learn to actually experience Creation again before time runs out.

The Four Lands of Heaven's Compass

Heaven's Compass will be our model of the psyche. With it, we will explore the powerful consequences of our split-brain. The

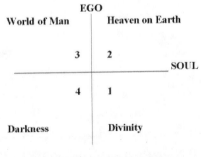

Image 1. Lands of the Religious Psyche

four Lands of the Religious Psyche portrayed in the modern creation story are now depicted below along with an explanation of the axes and a description of the contents of each land.

The vertical axis represents the ego or "I" part of the personality – the me that focuses consciousness, makes decisions, and wants to run the show. Descending the vertical axis, the "I" as ego steadily loses control of consciousness, until disappearing either into unconsciousness (via repression, intoxication, sleep, unconsciousness on the left side) or divinity (via dissolution of our separate consciousness into divine consciousness on the right side). Soul, the horizontal axis, represents our spiritual essence that enters the psyche to create and shape the true self. Moving from right to left on the horizontal axis represents the ego progressively losing touch with soul until the connection is gone.

Regarding the split-brain, the left side of the model represents *psychological* aspects of the personality that developed from our unfolding speech, language, and conceptual abilities, including thoughts, beliefs, feelings, inner conflicts, impulses, and so forth. The right side of the model refers to our non-language *mystical* aspects, including the direct experience of divinity as Self and Creation.

Below are descriptions of the essential qualities of each land. Though Creation begins in Quadrant 1, we begin our review in Quadrant 3, the World of Man, for it is here that we so profoundly lose our way.

The World of Man (Quadrant 3)

Quadrant 3 is made up of thoughts, ideas, and beliefs that are woven into complicated stories. These stories tell us who we are, what we should do, think and be, how the world works, and especially what's wrong with our lives. I've labeled it the World of Man because it is largely a man-made construction and because it's dominated by patriarchal values, like hierarchy, control, ownership, conflict, competition, productivity, and classification. An endless system of collective beliefs and assumptions, it is the origin and essence of duality, and it's where we get addicted to the dramas created by thought. While science, history, philosophy, theology, and other intellectual disciplines are also found here, these systems still represent maps that – no matter how helpful – separate us from direct experience.

Central to this land is the false self – who we *think* we are – that generates constant worries about personal worth, love, security, and survival. We ask, "Am I good enough, smart enough, attractive enough, or rich enough?" We might just as well call this "the land of worried thoughts" because its beliefs stir up so much fear, doubt, envy, competition and self-criticism. This is also the home of goals and ambitions, for here we believe that if we try hard enough, we can solve our self-made problems and ultimately achieve lasting worth and security. In actuality, Quadrant 3 is a fantasyland of stories and beliefs, an addictive mental template overlaid on the divine world. Favoring thought over perception, we lose Creation and achieve instead the imaginary world of the mind.

The problems bedeviling humanity are created in this land of endless and often conflicting thought forms. Blinded by the false self's greed, self-serving beliefs, delusions of grandeur, and short-sighted consciousness, we pursue the feel-good drugs of power and wealth; objectify, stereotype and devalue others; trash the Earth; and cause untold injuries to all who stand in the way of the raging freight train of opinions. With an easily corrupted conscience, minimally awakened consciousness, and attachment to emotional convictions over science, we fail to understand our behavior or manage its consequences.

Darkness (Quadrant 4)

The anxious, self-critical stories we tell in Quadrant 3 make us feel inadequate and inferior, which in turn causes anger, sadness, depression and shame. Since the World of Man is typically disapproving and impatient with these feelings, viewing them as signs of weakness, failure, self-pity or incivility, we bury them in the Darkness inside where we hide forbidden or unwanted thoughts and emotions, creating a shadow self of "unacceptable" feelings. Quadrant 4 could thus be called the "land of hurt and angry feelings" because it stores all the pain and unhappiness created by our "never good enough" beliefs. We also bury much of our true self here – who we were born to be, the very incarnation of the soul – because we're told it's not good enough. This inner Darkness becomes the unconscious when our true self and its feelings are hidden so well that even we can't remember them. Finally, moving in the depths of this underworld is our original grief – the child's self-inflicted pain of betraying our divine nature and the experience of Heaven on Earth to fit properly into the World of Man.

Quadrant 4 also contributes to the collective problems of today, creating Hell on Earth with its suffering, endless competition for wealth, and war. From this land, we lash out at those we can blame, breeding racism, sexism, hate crimes, religious and ethnic conflict. With neither psychological insight nor healing, we hurt others as we are hurt, fuel the World of Man's prejudices, and maintain the endless cycle of violence.

On the positive side, psychological healing begins in Quadrant 4 when we understand and work through the personal hurt stored there through compassionate friendships, psychotherapy and spiritual direction, journaling and self-reflection, and revision of our Quadrant 3 negative beliefs and thought processes.

Divinity (Quadrant 1)

Quadrant 1 is the home of the divine and its consciousness. Coming into this timeless space awakens a deep sense of stillness, peace, love, relaxation, and happiness. This realm could also be called the "land of pure joy" because of the feelings evoked whenever we experience the divine Presence. Time spent in this consciousness dissolves worried thoughts, fantasies and the problems they seem to create. As we go deeper into the experience of divinity, our constructs of a separate self and separate world dissolve. Here there is no you, no world, no thought, and no form at all, only the single pure unchanging experience of divine consciousness beyond space and time. Going further still, a personal sense of consciousness sometimes disappears altogether as we are swept into the light. This land is also known as the Self: the divine consciousness secreted inside our own consciousness and representing our truest nature. It is the source of all that is and our deepest wisdom. Lastly, we also enter Quadrant 1 through spiritual practices, spontaneous mystical experiences, holy places, great beauty, the "zone" of athletic competition, and the practice of mystical consciousness.

In this land, the healing process accelerates. We dissolve feelings of inferiority, invidious comparisons, fear of failure, even the dread of death, for here there is nothing to do, no place to go, and no one to be, fail or die. Here there is only the One and its infinite loving bliss, and we open its unconditional love secreted in our depths and in the experience of Presence.

Heaven on Earth (Quadrant 2)

In Quadrant 2, the divine has become the world and the world is a sacred place. This land is variously called Creation, the Garden of Eden, the Garden of Shiva, Heaven on Earth, and countless other names. Whatever its name, this realm appears whenever the awakened experience of Presence joyously transfigures ordinary reality into a radiant wonderland. Quadrant 2 could just as well be called the "land of wonder and love" because everything is seen as it truly is: infinitely perfect, pristine, amazing, precious, loving and divine.

Here humanity's healing continues. Here we experience the Earth as our sacred home, ourselves as divine beings, and others as our family. We live in Garden consciousness and know that all are made of God. As evidenced in the mystical experiences described in Chapter 3, Quadrant 2 completely changes our experience of the world. If only people knew the joy of divine life, the mystics tell us, we would cease this foolish fighting over our illusions. The mystical consciousness of this realm also erases the projected thought forms of Quadrant 3 to reveal the world in its true radiance, beauty and sacred perfection. We are finally home. Now we as divine humans can use the divine gift of thought to build a new world, rather than competing for superiority and invincibility as false selves.

Heaven on Earth engenders a sense of unity experienced emotionally in our loving bonds with each other. When we feel close, safe, and connected to loved ones, life feels right and good. Conversely, when these emotional bonds are damaged or severed by beliefs and actions from Quadrant 3, we hurt deeply and experience distressing emotions like grief, sadness, anger and depression.

The specific contents of Heaven's Compass are summarized below:

EGO

World of Man	Heaven on Earth
Thoughts & Beliefs	*Reality Perceived in Mystical Consciousness*
Patriarchal Values	*Beauty, Radiance, Light*
Self Idea	*True Self w/o Self Idea*
False Self	*Divine Human*
Problems & Stories	*Flow and Being vs. Doing*
Goals & Ambitions	*Moment as Guru*
Duality (False World)	*Unity*
Ideas of Good & Evil	*Original Blessing*
Hell on Earth	*Divine as Reality*
Rules and Customs	*Freedom*
3	2

SOUL

4	1
Darkness	**Divinity**
Pain & Anger	*Joy & Ecstasy*
Betrayed True Self	*No Self, No World, No Problems*
Shadow	*Divine Self*
Body as Self	*Presence*
Personal Unconscious	*Ultimate Consciousness*
Personal Hell	*All-Pervading Love*
Diminished Awareness	*Pure Consciousness & Potentiality*
Psychological Side	**Mystical Side**

Image 2. Contents of the Religious Psyche

Before proceeding onward, spend some time imagining what you might experience in each land. How do you feel, what do you think, what does the world look like?

The Cycle of Spiritual Experience

We turn now to the second part of our compass metaphor: the journey we take through the lands of the Religious Psyche in our journey home. This cycle of experience has four fundamental movements: betrayal, descent, reunion and renewal (ascent). To help you recognize this cycle in your everyday life, put yourself in this little vignette.

It's a quiet Sunday afternoon. You are doing something you really love (reading, gardening, listening to music). There are no deadlines, problems or social expectations to impinge on this happy and carefree space. Imagine how much you are enjoying this activity, how your soul sings, and how the day feels timeless, precious and "just perfect." Life is beautiful! Where are you in Heaven's Compass? Yes, Heaven on Earth!

Imagine now that this free and blissful consciousness is interrupted by a telephone call from a coworker, relative or neighbor about something essentially unimportant. You force yourself to take the call and it goes on for over an hour while you try to act interested and polite. Having abandoned your true self and its joy, you put on your "good" false self. You even convinced yourself that it was a "good" and "productive" talk. Where are you now in Heaven's Compass? Right, the World of Man.

Finally, the phone call is over. Think back to earlier in the day. What became of your original contentment, creativity and joy? What do you feel instead – numbness, emptiness, restlessness, irritability, depression? Having severed true self from soul and twisted it into a false self, you inflicted a personal wound and then quickly buried it inside. You could continue suppressing the pain of this betrayal by keeping busy or discharging it indirectly by being cranky with others. Instead, you let yourself simply feel the underlying hurt and disappointment and respond to these feelings with kindness and empathy. Imagine that you even have a good cry. Where are you now in Heaven's Compass? Yes, you entered the Darkness within.

Imagine now that you rest quietly in the stillness and silence that naturally follow a good cry. It is a peaceful, timeless, silent space, free of thought, struggle or goals. Without knowing it, you are being further healed by doing nothing at all, simply resting in the silence and stillness. Feel, too, the deep healing in your own body. With no self-concept or emotional tension, your physical being has relaxed and reunites naturally with the omnipresent divine being. Where are you now in Heaven's Compass? You are resting in the consciousness and being of divinity.

As you rest in this deep quiet, imagine waiting patiently for new inspiration or desire to arise. Take your time, don't rush it. Then, suddenly, you know just what you want to do, what would now feel really good. Perhaps it is a return to your original activity or something else you love. As you begin anew, notice the energy, motivation and joy that return, meaning the soul's nature is once again filling the true self with its essence. Don't start thinking about this, instead dissolve awareness in the deeply satisfying flow of whatever you are doing and let it flow. Surrender to the simple beauty and joy of being alive. Where are you now in Heaven's Compass? You have returned to the consciousness of Heaven on Earth.

This core cycle of Heaven's Compass is pictured overleaf.

One final caveat here. A phone call from anyone, no matter how superficial it may seem, may still reflect that person's suffering and need, so it is important to care for the true selves of both. The struggle here is partly developmental – in the beginning, we betray ourselves so easily with interruptions and distractions that we fail to make and hold sacred space for deep self-contact. As we grow our capacity to "care of the soul," we

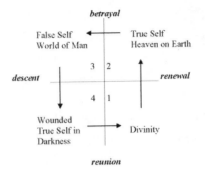

Image 3. The Cycle of Spiritual Life

find ways to balance the needs of both self and other; unplugging the phone for some quiet space might have been a solution!

The Seasons and Cycles of Spiritual Life

It is interesting to note that, on a much larger scale, this same sequence also moves us through the seasons and cycles of life. Here's a description of the three major rounds: The Personal Life, the Transpersonal Life, and the Mystical Life. These larger cycles carry us like tides between the psychological and mystical pulls of the personality.

In Cycle 1, *The Personal Life*, we are birthed from Quadrant 1 into the divine world of Quadrant 2, and experience the magic and enchantment of early childhood. By the age of seven, however, we are increasingly absorbed into Quadrant 3, the World of Man, constructing a personal identity, early wounds, vague heroic quest, and enduring story to carry us through adolescence and young adulthood into the summer of life. By midlife, our personal world has filled with problems and demands, for we have traveled far from the original vision of our soul. Indeed, in the Midlife Passage, we question the whole project of achievement, performance, acquisition and ever-increasing responsibility.

In our grief and frustration, we begin to dig deep inside,

reaching down into Quadrant 4 for the person we lost on the road to "success." If we do this skillfully, we recover the true self and its gifts. In the silence of waiting, on long afternoon walks, we intuitively long for what's been missing all this time – true self, soul, and Creation. Often, we are not fully conscious of this turn toward the divine but aware that something new is calling us. In this reconnecting process, we move naturally into Quadrant 1 to fill again with the soul's vision. Then, if we are patient, we will be "born again" in the Fall of life in Quadrant 2, drawn now to do the work of our soul.

In Cycle 2, *The Transpersonal Life*, we sense a spiritual vision that transcends the collective goals of society and tap into higher spiritual energies. In small or big ways, we finally return to what we love, what we came here to do, moving again into Quadrant 2. In time, Fall gives way to Winter in Quadrant 3, a time of aging, where we – like trees losing their leaves – gradually surrender all we thought we were: identity, social roles, appearance, physical vitality, and unending time span. In this process, we move down again into Quadrant 4, grieving what will never be again. Experiencing this great emptying, however, we discover that what's left is consciousness itself, which turns out to be the consciousness of divinity, and we open again into Quadrant 1.

Cycle 3 begins *The Mystical Life*. In the transformed consciousness of the *Late Life Passage*, we rediscover the mystical consciousness in Heaven on Earth. Those of us who understand and welcome these changes become enlightened elders, bodhisattvas and divine humans. Our work then is to awaken the World of Man's collective consciousness, dissolving the split psyche and merging secular and sacred, Heaven and Earth, human and divinity. We now find the wisdom inherent in transformed consciousness and, using thought in divinely inspired ways, create a new kind of humanity and a new kind of world. We also move from mystic to prophet, for the soul begins to reveal its deep activism and insists that we offer our sacred gifts to the world.

Conclusions

Play with this model. Draw its quadrants and try to place the parts of your life into each one. Describe your false self, the false world of rules and expectations you live in, the deepest feelings of your true self, the way you experience divinity, and times when the world feels like Heaven on Earth. Reflect, too, on how you may have experienced the cycles we've discussed, providing a map for your own journey. Fill in the quadrants with your observations of the world. What goes on in each quadrant?

You may find yourself asking, "Where is God?" in humanity's unfolding climate nightmare. The answer, provided by Heaven's Compass, is revealing. Notice that there is no common permeable boundary in Heaven's Compass between the World of Man and Divinity; they are so separate as to be totally disconnected. In other words, Divinity is always here but the World of Man is so insulated, self-contained and self-absorbed that it is completely oblivious to Divinity's actual presence. No matter how much we may talk about God, we don't truly experience the divine in the World of Man.

So far, we have explored the nature of the world's crisis, the importance of moving from personal spirituality to an awakened vision of Creation, and the journey we take through the seasons and cycles of life to come home to Heaven on Earth. In *Part II, Mystical Transformation*, we open the consciousness of the divine human to know who and where we really are in preparation for the work of *Part III, Mystical Activism*. This journey can change your life and help transform the world.

Part II

Mystical Transformation: Healing the Divided Psyche

Chapter 5

Presence: Awakening Mystical Consciousness

The experience of Presence is the doorway to mystical consciousness. You have stumbled into it countless times. Now we want to make the experience of Presence intentional.

What Is Presence?

Presence refers to the immediate and tangible experience of God's consciousness in the world, in our consciousness, and in our physical being. A personal, subjective, here-and-now, one-of-a-kind encounter with, and immersion in, the divine, it is the source and essence of mystical consciousness. This chapter describes the awareness, qualities and dynamics of Presence. In learning to experience Presence, we awaken the powers of the mystic.

How Do We Sense Presence?

Presence is located most distinctly in the stillness, silence, and timelessness that pervade everything in the present moment. It is often associated with the realization that space itself is conscious and alive.

Locating this Presence involves the sharpening and heightening of awareness. The immediacy and aliveness of surrounding space is sensed with a keen, penetrating and thought-free awareness, as if trying to "feel" the energy of another person in a pitch-black room. The only difference is that we are sensing the aliveness of space itself. The Presence we discover is beyond thought, beliefs, feelings, images or imaginings. It is not something we conjure up nor is it found through visualization or active imagination exercises. Rather, Presence must be encountered directly as a real and unmistakable consciousness pervading all space and reality.

We spontaneously experience Presence in the awe, wonder, and reverence evoked by nature's grandeur, sacred sites, or powerful rituals. Holding our attention, we know, if only for a moment, that we are literally in the Presence of God. We also come into Presence through prayer, meditation or the mystical consciousness, practices in which we intentionally seek contact with the divine. Presence is frequently discernable in extraordinary times, like childbirth, danger, and the passage of death, when consciousness awakens spontaneously and the sacred preciousness of life is suddenly undeniable. Finally, though we may not realize it, the timeless experience of Presence can permeate consciousness during intense activities, like sports, dance and creativity when the mind is free of thought and filled with the spontaneous and unconstrained energy of active being some call the "zone." Once we learn how to sense Presence, however, we can find it everywhere. Then we have begun what the mystics call the "Practice of Presence."

Qualities and Dynamics of Presence

Though the experience of Presence seems to come and go, in reality it is our awareness of it that vacillates. It is especially elusive when we are upset, rushed, or pursuing ego-inflating projects, plans and schemes, hence the unconscious and unconscionable behavior found in the World of Man. In fact, awareness of Presence can be lost or forgotten for years at a time.

It may be startling at first to realize that space is alive and aware, but with time, this notion becomes familiar and comforting. Like any new relationship, there is an initial period devoted to meeting, getting acquainted, and exploring the relationship until it feels familiar, comfortable, trustworthy, and intimate. Once located, people may describe Presence as sweet, intimate, gentle, loving, forgiving, unconditional, uncritical, accepting, and patient. It is never tired, disinterested, frustrated, or angry. Always waiting for us, Presence is the ultimate intimacy, empathy, and mercy.

Entering this Presence, we often notice an increase in ambient light. Falling gently on things nearby, the light of Presence renders everything more beautiful, bright, crystal clear, and fascinating. The world is subtly but wonderfully transfigured in its soft and celestial illumination, which is, itself, the Presence.

As we let Presence come closer, surrounding and touching us like the warm softness of a blanket, we begin to feel peaceful, content, relaxed, and safe. There is no fear, time urgency, or worry in this loving and protected space. Moreover, experiencing this closeness and unity with Presence often evokes immense joy, which some describe as the soul's response to its reunion and renewed intimacy with God.

We are often moved to spontaneity in Presence. Whether in dance, song, creativity, service, lovemaking, or even mundane activities like cleaning or yard work, when Presence surrounds, enters, or awakens us, whatever we do is transformed into a flowing, joyous, generous, unpremeditated, and even sacred process. In emergencies, too, we may be moved by Presence to perform acts transcending our normal fears about personal safety.

Spending time in Presence changes us, making us more like the Presence itself. Increasingly, we take on its nature: calm, serene, patient, accepting, kind, and aware of the beauty and value of everyday life, the world, and all living things. Time in Presence is also healing. Cradled in the experienced kindness of God, we recognize the error of our self-centered ways and our violent emotions gradually melt away. Upsets are seen for what they are: misunderstandings that are temporary, self-created, and misleading. Holding every human drama is always the holiness of presence, a sanctuary we can return to anytime.

Presence does not "fix" our life dramas in the conventional

sense; rather, it profoundly changes our perception of them. Time, story, and the soap-opera quality of life all disappear in Presence. In divine consciousness, life is not a linear sequence of past, present, and future, a problem to be solved, or a goal to be reached; it is the eternal "now" opening like a flower into the mystical experience of being.

Consciousness filled with Presence is the source of all genuine and spiritually enlightened action. From its depths flow the most authentic and loving responses we can have to the people and situations of our lives. We become better people in the experience of Presence.

Presence is also something we share with each other. This is one of its most powerful gifts, for being in Presence together magnifies all its qualities. Then, peace, joy, compassion, and love not only melt the divisions between us, they flow through us into the world. This is the most powerful source of social action.

Presence is not an achievement to be had, put away, and kept like a possession, souvenir or pressed flower, nor is it a belief we cling to for comfort and security. It is the always new, fresh and unfolding opening into the divine. As such, it is the source, essence and awakening of a life divine.

Presence is timeless and unchanging. It is the same Presence experienced by Buddha, Jesus, Mohammad, and Lao-tzu. It is the same Presence you will know, and the one your great-great-grandchildren will know. Presence is the pervasive, unchanging, and infinite consciousness in which the entire human drama of time and history are enacted. In fact, in the consciousness of Presence, time and history do not exist. Humankind's images and understanding of the divine, however, change in the World of Man over the millennia, colored by the psychology, culture, reality beliefs and personal experiences of those who describe it. The contradictions found within and between religions arise from these factors as well as our inherently limited capacity to comprehend the fullness of Divinity.

Because fully knowing Divinity is beyond the capacity of the human mind, we experience it in many discrete and sometimes contradictory forms, including a personal and imminent Presence, a transcendent entity beyond the world, the pure consciousness in which everything arises, an impersonal force recognized through its orderliness as described by scientific laws, a void from which everything forms and returns, and existence itself as divine being. Ironically, these beliefs and their contradictions become unimportant in the Presence, for it is God that we meet, not our ideas of God. And, as we will see, our experience of the divine is in fact quite different in each quadrant of Heaven's Compass, often adding to our collective confusion.

Presence shows us what God is and, by extension, what we are. Eventually, we realize that our own presence is actually part of, one with, and the same as *the* Presence – sacred consciousness seemingly distributed individually yet always one. Awareness of one's own presence, therefore, can also be a doorway into Presence, for as the mystics across religions attest in Chapter 7, Presence is our truest essence. As personal boundaries dissolve, Presence is all that remains.

Finally, the experience of Presence is central to the mystical experience, for it is this direct, firsthand experience of the divine that transfigures reality, surrounds us with love, and opens the perceptual gates to the radiant splendor of Heaven on Earth. And while mystics, saints and the very devout have referred to Presence for centuries, few have left us with practical instructions for directly experiencing it.

Experiencing Presence

Here is an exercise for entering and experiencing the Presence, activating on the four Keys to Mystical Consciousness described in Chapter 3, and moving toward the state of mystical union. Follow the directions slowly with plenty of time between each instruction to open perception to the experiential dimensions described. As the experience deepens, you may wish to stop and digest what has happened before continuing or start over to go deeper.

Preparation

1. Sit in a quiet, peaceful place undistracted by music, television, noises or others. Be sure you have enough time to forget about time.

2. Cease all activity. Become quiet, still and centered. Take a few deep breaths and let go of any worries, plans or schedule concerns. Let your thoughts slow down and settle to rest, and try not to analyze or manipulate this experience. In other words, be here now and experience the moment exactly as it is. But don't close your eyes and don't get dreamy. This is about waking up.

3. Intensify and sharpen your awareness, perceiving everything around you with crystal clarity. Look at the world as if for the very first time – new, fresh, unfamiliar, and fascinating. Be filled with awe at the beauty of Creation.

4. Select something close to you as a focal point for your vision, like your hand, a pencil, or the fabric of your clothing. Look at it with intense perceptual clarity. Notice its colors, pattern, and texture, and experience its depth, beauty and perfection. Notice how the light plays on it. See it exactly as it is without thought. This is pure perception. Be amazed!

5. As you hold your gaze on your focal point, become aware of the space around you at the same time. Experience it in the same heightened, clarified, thoughtless awareness.

You are very close to the sensing Presence.

Sensing Presence

6. Staying on your focal point, probe the surrounding space with your peripheral heightened consciousness. See if you can feel or perceive another awareness, not your own, filling that space. Sense space itself as awake and aware, and that you are surrounded by consciousness.

7. You might whisper or silently say something like, "God, I know you are here, I sense you," or simply repeat your name for divinity several times, inviting connection and sensing what happens in the room as you do so.

8. Notice how you begin to sense space or reality filling with the gentle aliveness of Presence. With your eyes still on your focal point, keep exploring your sense of divine space until you actually experience this other consciousness in some way. Don't think about what is happening, focus on divine consciousness everywhere and intensify your awareness of it.

9. See if you can notice now that this surrounding consciousness knows you and is aware that you are aware of it. Focus on this direct experience of mutual knowing. It is the first step in developing a conscious relationship with this Presence.

10. Now feel the energy of Presence close to you, within a few inches of your body. As you experience this closeness, it may begin to feel warm, gentle, kind, intimate, and loving.

Entering Presence

11. Sense yourself surrounded, touched and known by this loving invisible consciousness. You may actually feel it warming the room, caressing your skin, or flowing over your being.

12. Come further into the Presence the way you would come into the presence of another person, by relaxing and accepting the experience of communion. Feel its energy and tune into its loving nature. Trust what you sense.

13. Allow yourself to be drawn further into loving communion through conversation. Talk slowly, silently, and intimately with the Presence, sharing your life, feelings, prayers, anything you'd like. Let your heart and soul be touched by this One that holds you so tenderly.

14. Take a few moments to further explore your relationship with Presence. For example, notice what happens in this process when you express love, praise, or gratitude. Do your feelings affect Presence? Does being in this Presence change or affect you?

15. Continue in this very subjective, experiential process as long as it feels real and helpful. Be careful not to lose Presence by thinking about what is happening, and don't lapse into fantasy. Remember, this experience is beyond ideas, beliefs and imaginings, and it can come and go depending on your awareness. You may sense Presence, lose it, then sense it again. There is an art to staying in the consciousness of God, and you will learn to perfect it for yourself.

Letting Presence Enter You

16. Now sense your own consciousness and realize that the consciousness you locate inside is also God's consciousness. Sense it moving into your physical being, saturating it with the feeling, energy, and divine consciousness. Notice how you can actually move it through your body by moving your attention.

17. Notice, too, how an experience of union is beginning in this merging: your presence becoming one with the Presence, your being becoming one with divine being. As you feel this oneness, gratefully relinquish your separate, worried, problem-ridden self in the divine Other.

18. Feel the joy, relief, and freedom that accompany giving up the burden of self and identity, allowing the Presence to be your presence. It is not that you alone are God or that God has commandeered your personality or that you now have all God's power – these are all foolish stories that keep us from this union – only that pure consciousness and being are the experience of God.

19. Here is one final optional step. Stand up. Begin walking slowly, consciously, very deliberately, fully present, feeling God flowing through your movements, thoughts, and perceptions. Live this moment as the Presence living you, learning to live from the divine Self instead of the personal self. This is where your mystical activism will eventually take place.

20. When you are ready, take a deep breath, come back into your ordinary experience of self and body, and sit quietly for a few minutes reflecting on what you experienced. Describe the experience in your journal. Later you can

compare it with other experiences and see how your mystical skills have progressed. Because your mystical sensitivity will increase with practice, look for success – moments of awakening consciousness – and resist negative thoughts that try to undermine your experience. You will have many opportunities to practice this skill in the pages ahead.

Developing a Daily Relationship with Presence

If you are interested in going deeper, create an ongoing relationship with Presence by spending time in it every day. Your communion will evolve and deepen with practice. Here are some additional things to consider in this process:

- Be sure to take care of this relationship. Like any valued friendship, its authenticity and depth depend on the continuing respect, sincerity, and genuine attention you bring to it.
- Enter Presence whenever you are hurt, confused, or off balance – when you need to prepare for something difficult or make a tough decision. See how it changes your entire orientation to the problem facing you. Be sure to take your time, have no expectations, and make no demands. Let Presence change you.
- As you "practice Presence" over time, notice what contributes to finding, losing and finding it again in your daily life.
- Notice, too, how you are changing. What do you discover about your own nature in the process? What is Presence teaching you?

What Presence is Not

Remember: Presence is real. It is not visualization, imagination, self-improvement or an attempt to get God to change something, nor is it simply a "feel good," need-gratifying technique to relax or escape from pain. Practicing Presence is its own end: a melting into the peace and serenity of eternity beyond the world's concern for efficiency, productivity, and success. Though Presence may transform your life, sometimes even produce extraordinary changes, results are not the reason we come into this sacred dimension. It is divinity alone that we seek. However your life changes, or doesn't change, matters little. Rest in Presence and then return to the world with gratitude, seeing that it, too, is surrounded and permeated by Presence. Everything follows naturally from here.

Presence comprises the essence of mystical consciousness, for they are actually one and the same. In other words, mystical consciousness is divine consciousness. This state of consciousness will transform your perception, personality and place in the world, revealing Heaven on Earth, your nature as a divine human, the potential of mystical activism, and the gifts you came here to share. You are heading into a profoundly transformational process.

Chapter 6

Finding Heaven Here: Where We Really Live

We live in a divine world. I mean that literally. Heaven is already here when we're awake enough to see it. This is probably the biggest secret on the spiritual path! We never left the Garden, we just forgot how to see it. We expelled ourselves.

What Mystics Teach Us About Heaven on Earth

The mystics have been telling us about Heaven on Earth for centuries. Here is a sampling of their universal teaching:

Jesus said: "The father's kingdom is spread out upon the earth and people do not see it... What you look for has come, but you do not know it." Ramana Maharshi, the famous Hindu sage, added, "This is the Kingdom of Heaven. The realized being sees this as the Kingdom of Heaven whereas the others see it as 'this world.'" Thich Nhat Hanh, the beloved Buddhist monk, told us, "You don't have to die in order to enter the Kingdom of God. It is better to do it now when you are fully alive... The Kingdom doesn't have to come and you do not have to go to it. It is already here...There is not one day that I do not walk in the Kingdom of God." Faitel Levin, a rabbi, confided, "... this reality is transparent to its true being – the essence of this reality is nothing but the Essence of G-d." Li Po, a Taoist poet, wrote, "There is another heaven and earth beyond the world of men." Finally, Elizabeth Barrett Browning, an English poet, described, "Earth's crammed with heaven and every common bush alive with God."

So how do we make sense of these astonishing claims from Christian, Hindu, Buddhist, Jewish, Taoist, and poetry teachers? Eckhart Tolle explains, "A 'new heaven' is the emergence of a transformed state of human consciousness." That's an important clue. What is this consciousness? Over 100 years ago, Richard Bucke called it, "Cosmic Consciousness," and said that the person experiencing it "is lifted out of his old self and lives rather in heaven than upon the old earth – more correctly the old earth becomes heaven." Joseph Campbell, the renowned scholar of religion and mythology, eloquently summed up, "This is it. This is Eden. When you see the kingdom spread upon the earth, the old way of living in the world is annihilated. That is the end of the world. The end of the world is not an event to come, it is an event of psychological transformation, of visionary transformation. You see not the world of solid things but a world of radiance." But Benedictine author, Joan Chittister, may have said it best, "Am I going to heaven? No, I am already there and it is getting more heavenly every day."

Why Don't We See Heaven on Earth?

If Heaven on Earth is all around us, why don't we see it? The answer is that we never stop to look! As we glance at things in the world, we either ignore them completely or automatically reduce them to the concepts and objects defined by the World of Man: car, tree, person, movie, pencil, bird. We label what we see and quickly move past. Without realizing it, we have imprisoned ourselves in a mental world that instantly replaces perception with conception – ideas, beliefs, explanations, and opinions. Because our thought world provides the illusion of certainty, security, and consensual agreement, we never question it. But let's question it now.

Finding Heaven Here – An Experience of the Divine World

Finding Heaven on Earth cannot be an intellectual exercise. Because we need to see it directly, for ourselves, let's begin this time with an experiential exercise. The exercise has two steps.

First, go outside and consciously select and bring back a natural object – a leaf, pinecone, twig, rock, dirt clod, flower, whatever, something that fits easily into your hand.

This exercise is an experiment in the mystical consciousness of the divine world. Don't worry about doing it perfectly. Don't worry about whether anything is happening. Don't try to figure it out. Just follow the directions and notice what you notice. Take all the time you need, go slowly, and experience the sensory qualities described in the instructions. Ready? Here goes...

1. Keep your eyes open throughout the experiment. You can't see the divine world with your eyes closed! And remember, this is not meditation, guided imagery, or spontaneous fantasy. In fact, it may be different from anything you've done before.

2. Take a moment to quiet your mind. Let your thoughts slow down and unwind. Get comfortable in your chair, centered in your own personal space and physical being. Focus attention on the sensory perception of the immediate here-and-now.

3. Now, slowly, consciously and deliberately, pick up the object you brought in from outside and place it on your lap or hold it in your hands. Let it be your visual focal point for the exercise. Just keep gazing at the object.

4. While you're looking at the object, listen to the silence in the room and sense the stillness of the present moment that is everywhere. Simply sit quietly in this stillness gazing at your object. Anytime your thoughts resume, remind yourself to stop thinking and return to silence and stillness as you gaze ever more deeply at the piece of nature you brought in.

5. Now in this still and conscious moment, I want you to heighten and sharpen your senses even more. Once again, become as alert, awake and aware as you possibly can. Wake up!

6. Heighten this awareness even further by opening the awe response. You already know what awe feels like. You felt it when you stood in rapt attention as a child gazing up at the night sky or, as an adult, down at your newborn infant. That intense, wide-eyed, breath-catching, thought-free awareness. Awaken that intense consciousness as you expand your sense of awe.

7. Now, focus your vision and this intense awareness again on the item you brought in from outside. Carefully examine its visual properties: its colors, pattern, and texture. Experience its depth, beauty and perfection. Notice how the light plays on it. Smell it. Touch it. Feel it on your face. Look deeply into it with your soul. Love it. Merge with it. See it exactly as it is without thought. This is pure perception. See it as if you've never seen anything so clearly before. Be amazed.

8. Keep looking at the object. As you gaze at it, become aware of your own consciousness, in other words, become conscious of consciousness itself, remembering that all consciousness is divine consciousness. Keep gazing at the object with this pure awareness. See if you can sense that divine consciousness now exists all around you, as if space itself has become alive and aware. Just notice.

9. This heightened state of mystical consciousness may further change your perception of the object you picked. It may seem brighter, even more beautiful, more

interesting, more radiant, more alive, and it is, because you are dissolving the lens of thought that separates you from the divine world. Everything now is infinitely beautiful, infinitely precious, perfect, enchanting, radiant, shimmering with light, conscious, alive, and full of love. The divine world is still here, you are looking at it, you are looking into it. You knew this world as a child, you can find it again as a conscious adult. Be amazed. Be grateful. Take your time to absorb this profound revelation. You are in deep communion with divine being as the world itself.

10. When you're ready, bring yourself back to normal everyday consciousness. Move around a little, sit up, and reconnect with your customary self-experience. Get the operating system of your mind back online, as the computer guys might say, so you can reflect on this experience in your journal.

Journaling Reflections

Here are some specific questions for reflection. It's often helpful to write your responses in your journal to understand your experience more completely.

- What happened for you in this experience?
- Did your perception of the object change?
- Did your consciousness change in any way?
- How did the exercise make you feel?
- As you focused on the object, did you notice how incredibly beautiful it became? Were you enchanted by it? How?
- Staring at it intently, could you sense a larger consciousness around you? What was that like?
- After the exercise, did your perception of the room change? How?

When I lead people through this exercise, many are awed by their encounter with the divine world. They begin to experience a deep communion, enchantment, love and compassion for the living conscious reality in their hands. The plant comes alive, opens before their eyes, communicates with them, touching their heart and growing ever more beautiful. Their feelings about the world temporarily change. They know something important has happened and they themselves feel changed. The challenge then lies in maintaining this perceptual openness before falling back into the automatic labeling in the World of Man. But they remember. And, recognizing the profound importance of this transformation, some begin to practice mystical consciousness to awaken this kind of seeing more often.

A Walk in Heaven on Earth

I often walk from my house to the end of a spit on the island where I live. One day, I recorded my experience in this awakened right-hemisphere consciousness. I use words to describe and communicate this experience because they are necessary, but they do not replace what I experienced. Here is my ambling experience.

I am acutely awake, alert, and present. Consciousness is free of thought and judgment. Awareness is wide open, silent and still, taken over by sheer curiosity, enchantment, wonder, amazement and radical awe. With no distracting self-idea, I am immersed in a glorious always-new landscape. With the vivid freshness of sensory experience, the woods are exquisitely beautiful, colorful, luminous, and steeped in an ambience of holiness. I sense that everything here is alive and intensely conscious, even inanimate objects, and every "thing" invites me further into this numinous realm no matter how small or seemingly inconsequential.

Moving fluidly, untroubled, unafraid, I feel a deep and permeating sense of peace, calm, and trust in the goodness of this steadily opening mystery. With no self, there are no problems, agendas or goals and my movements are unscripted, unplanned, and unprogrammed. It's a state of absolute freedom, no rules, no boundaries, no expectations, just flowing, wild, spontaneous, glorious, awakening life.

My energy is friendly, optimistic, hopeful, and I radiate love, joy and gratitude as my heart opens ever wider. Each moment is timeless, unending and forever, with no past, present or future. Dissolved in the profound experience of unity, I feel so grateful. I want to merge with everything, roll in the sand, and inhale the perfume of dirt, grass and water. And most amazingly, I realize again that this divine and magical kingdom is always here, always just a shift in consciousness away, the imminent divine, Heaven on Earth. Inspired by this expanding consciousness, I want to say to people, "Stop, be silent, wake up. You are not who, what or where you think. See what I see. We have another home in divinity."

You might try the same experiment. Use the above exercise to awaken your own mystical perception and then take a walk in nature. Walk slowly, peacefully, without intention, thought or goals, and simply notice things. Be enchanted by the experience. Meet each life form as uniquely embodied divine consciousness. Commune with each "being" you meet. Then write your own description of "A Walk in Heaven on Earth."

Evidence for Heaven on Earth is right before our eyes. As Thomas Berry reminded us, "The universe is a communion of subjects, not a collection of objects." We are all one living consciousness moving through countless temporary forms. We need only wake up enough to see and know this, and then to better know ourselves.

Chapter 7

The Divine Human: Who We Really Are

What do the mystics tell us about our own divinity? Let's hear from them again. Because they come from a state of divine consciousness, their words have the power to awaken your own divinity. Read them slowly. Read them several times. Read them out loud. Notice how they affect you. Invite these possibilities inside yourself.

What the Mystics Teach Us About the Divine Human

The Christian mystic Meister Eckhart said, "In my soul, God not only gives birth to me as His son, He gives birth to me as Himself, and Himself as me... Our truest I is God." From the Muslim religion, Ibn al-'Arabi added, "He who knows himself understands that his Existence is not his existence, but his Existence is the existence of God." The Buddhist Huang Po stated, "We forget that as soon as our thoughts are at peace and all attempts at forming ideas subside, then the Buddha is revealed." Thomas Merton, a popular Christian writer, confirmed, "If I find God I will find myself, and if I find myself, I will find God." From the Hindu perspective, Vivekananda wrote, "While we recognize a God, it is really only the Self that we have separated from ourselves and worship as outside us; but all the time it is our own true Self, the one and only God." Hildegard of Bingen exclaimed, "I am the fiery life of God." Finally, Zen writer Alan Watts summarized, "At any rate, the point is that God is what nobody admits to being, and everybody really is."

How are you affected by these teachers' words? Which mystic speaks directly to you? Repeat these phrases again, "If I find God, I will find myself. If I find myself, I will find God." "I am the fiery life of the essence of God." How do these words make you feel?

This is every mystic's essential message: We are already divine, we have simply forgotten how to experience it.

What is the Divine Human?

The Divine Human is someone who experiences body, self and the world as literally divine. It's a state of consciousness free of identity, time and story, and the whole problem-ridden labyrinth of left-brain thinking that dominates our lives. In mystical awareness, we experience our "own" consciousness and being as the consciousness and being of God.

Because this experience of being a Divine Human is nothing like you can imagine, and nothing like what's depicted in popular culture, don't imagine anything. Don't think about it because you'll just get tangled up in questions and arguments – in other words, more left-brain tyranny. We are moving from the left side of Heaven's Compass to the right side and our goal is the direct, firsthand *experience* of our divinity. You can't figure this out and the mind won't solve this problem; instead, let the consciousness of divinity become what you are.

How do we become a Divine Human in a Divine World?

Becoming a Divine Human is a three-stage process. We begin by understanding what the mystics have been telling us all along about our divinity and taking it seriously; then we engage spiritual practices to awaken the actual experience of our divine nature; and, finally, we allow this experience of divinity to progressively remake our personality and behavior, and that part is up to us.

But keep this in mind. To discover the divine self and the divine world, we have to temporarily dissolve every concept and image we have about our self, the world and God, otherwise we'll stay in the prison of thought preventing our transformation. We can learn how to do this! Let's start now.

Exercise: Awakening the Mystical Experience of the Divine Human

I invite you now to experience a little bit of your own divinity. This is a profound experience that can begin to awaken a sense of the inner divine. Again, have no expectations. Don't try to figure this exercise out. Don't think about what is or is not happening. Just let yourself be open to surprise.

1. Become quiet, close your eyes and relax. Take a couple of deep breaths and settle comfortably into your chair, into your body. And take a moment to make a space inside for this process to really happen.

2. Let your thoughts slow down, unwind, untangle, and come to rest. Release all the questions and issues troubling your mind, and focus your attention deep inside, descending into the rich dark inner space of self and spirit.

3. Sense the deep silence and stillness of this inner space. Simply sit quietly in this silent stillness within. And any time your thoughts resume, remind yourself to stop thinking and return to silence and stillness within. Deep silence and stillness.

4. Now in this still and conscious moment, I want you to intensify your awareness. Become as alert, awake and aware as you can, and open your awareness to the subtle dimensions of your inner experience. Look around inside. Explore this extraordinary inner space.

5. Sanctify this inner space by awakening a sense of *awe*. Awe is always associated with the presence of the Sacred. Do that now. Be in awe of your inner experience as if

you're sensing something holy, because you are!

6. Now focus this heightened awe-inspired consciousness on itself. Become conscious of consciousness itself. That consciousness is the literal presence of the inner divine. It is God's consciousness. What do you notice? What do you sense?

7. Now silently, inside, say to yourself, *"This is God."* Wait a few seconds, see what you notice, and then say it again, *"This is God."* Say it again and sense its presence and nature. If the word "God" doesn't feel right, use any name you like for the divine from here on. Continue using this prompt. Notice what this statement evokes in you. This consciousness is divine consciousness, literally! What feelings, realizations or experiences arise inside? Look for subtle movements of awareness, insight or energy. Be patient. Wait. Just notice. Let it happen.

8. Now move this sacred consciousness through your body by focusing it in different places. Notice how it feels in your heart, your head, your eyes, in your mind. Notice also how this consciousness melts places of pain, rigidity, hardness or distress, gradually transforming your very nature. Let the idea of "you" dissolve in the experience of divinity's pure loving conscious Presence. Melt into it.

9. Now focus awareness on the pure energy of the body. Feel the being of your being, the ground of being, the energetic essence of your physical embodiment. Feel it now.

10. When you're ready, silently repeat this phrase: *"This is God's being."* What do you feel or sense? Say it again: *"This*

is God's being." Stay in the awe-filled sensory awareness of your physical being and see what you notice. Say it once again: *"This is God's being."* Or you can say, *"My being is God's being."*

11. Continue to repeat this prompt every few seconds, intensifying the experience of divine being, until something more begins to happen inside, perhaps a feeling of joy, sense of astonishment, sudden insight, swelling of love, or a transformation of consciousness. We are priming the pump of your divine nature. Take a minute to go deeper.

12. Any time you feel uncomfortable with this experience, let that fear go and return to the silent, peaceful, loving, divine stillness inside.

13. Now repeat this prompt, *"I am what God is."* Notice how the phrase makes you feel and how it intensifies your experience of yourself as a loving divine being. Feel the tide of love rising inside, for that is what God is!

14. Notice how your sense of self is evolving, as if your God nature were replacing you, becoming you, healing, softening and opening your real nature. You *are* the divine love you have been seeking all your life. You are filling with it. You can even repeat the prompt, *"I am God,"* and notice how that feels. But no judgment, analysis, thinking or fantasy, just the prompt and then your pure awareness of what happens inside.

15. What is happening in you is deep, profound, loving, and spacious. It is your truest nature rising up inside, full of joy, full of holiness, full of love. You are opening,

welcoming and experiencing the divine Self that rises like a tide within and between us.

16. Keep in mind that this is an evolving experience. We each do it in a way that is perfect for where we are in this moment of our lives. So, no judgment, no comparisons. Simply pay attention to what is happening and how it feels. That way, more will follow and you won't get stuck in self-criticism.

17. Before you stop, try to remember one specific thing that surprised, touched or excited you from this exercise.

18. Now, when you are ready, come back into everyday consciousness, move your body around a little to get back into it in the ordinary way, and bring your conventional mind back online. When it feels comfortable, open your eyes. But when you do, notice how different the world seems, that it seems brighter, more beautiful, colorful, luminous and sacred. Transformed perception is a natural part of awakening the divine revealing the radiance of Heaven on Earth. You are on the threshold of the visionary transformation Joe Campbell described earlier. When you're ready, open your journal.

Reflection: What's Happening in This Exercise?

Begin to journal about your experience. What happened for you? Describe your experience gently, tentatively, with an open mind. Look for surprises or glimpses of awakening consciousness. As you write about them, see if your understanding expands. What is the one thing you want to remember from this exercise? How do you feel now?

With these prompts, you are calling forth an experience that is already there, latent, potential, intuitive, waiting to be awakened just as the mystics say. These prompts are powerful because they are true. Instead of activating your left hemisphere's false self, you are calling forth your real nature and then evoking that experience.

If you are troubled by anything that happened in this experience, reflect back on our discussion of negative and judgmental thoughts in the Introduction. This is "forbidden" territory in some religions and their judgmental messages may still generate fear in your unconscious. Try to remember how you learned to be afraid to acknowledge your own divinity, explore why and how this happened, and give yourself positive supportive messages instead. Later you will learn powerful exercises to transform your thinking, so stay upbeat.

Finally, as discussed previously, these exercises implicitly engage the Keys to Mystical Consciousness described in Chapter 3 for their power and effectiveness. We now add a fifth mystical key – "Feel into the Being of your being" – which, because all being is divine Being, naturally awakens new energy and action possibilities for mystical activism.

As we awaken the consciousness of the divine human, we become enlightened beings in a mystically transformed world. Integrating divine consciousness with divine being, we release our left-brain personality to live and work from a deeper state of divine union. Interestingly, our awakening as divine humans is also part of humanity's new aging experience.

Chapter 8

Elders as Transformational Mystics: The New Aging

This chapter is for older people and also for anyone wondering what aging is really all about. I will be sharing with you some pretty amazing ideas about the new aging. Some of these ideas may be hard to believe at first, but keep your mind open. Don't let skepticism, doubt or fixed opinions prevent these possibilities from transforming your final stage of life. We are talking about the potential for a new kind of aging and a new kind of elder. We are talking about the very purpose of aging.

The New Aging

I have come into a new consciousness in aging – a mystical consciousness. I am living it and it is changing me. I'm not the same person I was a few short years ago. I believe this consciousness represents a precursor to a revolution in human aging. I want to introduce this new evolutionary stage to you and invite you to a reconsider everything you know about growing older.

We're living in an extraordinary and unprecedented time. For nearly all of recorded history, only one person in ten could hope to live to the age of 65. When Thomas Jefferson was around, half the population in America was under the age of 16. The average life span in 1900 was 45. With the medical and dietary advances in the last 100 years, however, nearly 80% of us in developing countries will live to be past 65 (in fact, if you reach 65, you can expect 16 more years for men and 19 for women). By 2030, folks over 65 will outnumber teens 2 to 1 and be a third of the US population. What was once reserved for a tiny fraction of folks – no wonder elders were honored! – is increasingly available to all of us. It's sometimes called the "Third Age." It's absolutely incredible. But what is this revolution in longevity for? Are we just hanging around waiting for the reaper? The answer, of course, is, "No!" As you will see, this new developmental stage in the human life cycle is unlike anything that came before.

Our new aging is driven by three powerful forces that will profoundly change our lives if we let them. They are secrets because nobody wants to talk about them. The media is completely focused on overcoming aging with creams, exercise, vitamins, hormones, cosmetic surgery, new jobs, new mates, and new cars, but that only works for a while. Aging wins. But that doesn't mean we lose; rather it means we have to surrender to this still secret but life-transforming process. Why?

Rabbi Schachter-Shalomi, the founder of Sage-ing International, tells us that, "Elderhood represents the crowning achievement of life," and Jean Houston adds, "The years beyond sixty, the years of our second maturity, may be evolution's greatest gift to humanity." And Carl Jung, that famous psychoanalyst, said that old age would not exist unless it had an evolutionary purpose. This is what we want to understand – how can aging be the crowning achievement of life, the greatest gift to humanity, and a purposeful stage of human evolution? Isn't it just about falling apart and dying?

Now here's a question – meant especially for those over 60 – that will take us right into the heart of this chapter: How much younger do you feel on the inside compared to how old you look in your latest photograph? Shocking, huh? What's the moral here? You're not what you look like. In fact, who you are inside is actually ageless and timeless. This is an extremely important clue. Something very different is happening. Aging is a disguise that hides an amazing and profound process of human spiritual evolution. Awesome, scary, relentless and mysterious, aging will not be denied, but it's not what you think and it's not who you are. Clean the slate – everything you know about aging may be wrong or outdated.

The Three Secrets of Aging

Like childhood, adolescence, and midlife, aging is a developmental stage in the human life cycle. But this new aging represents a new kind of aging, one we're still trying to understand for ourselves. And it appears that we continue to develop psychologically and spiritually as we age. This is not a time of stasis, retreat or simply decline. Rather, our new aging appears to be a profoundly transformational stage, a journey into a new dimension of life and consciousness that will affect not only ourselves but the world. Let's start looking at these three secrets of aging.

Each secret has within it a series of tasks and gifts, and each secret can be understood at psychological, spiritual and mystical levels. So, there's a lot going on here. Consider how these three secrets might remake your life as an enlightened elder.

Secret I. *Aging is an Initiation into an Extraordinary New Stage of Life.* The magic word here is Initiation. The secret tells us that the events and processes of aging – changing bodies, fading identities, and losses of all shapes and sizes – represent an initiation into an entirely new dimension of life, a time of personal and spiritual growth unprecedented in human history. While aging may represent the end of our old life, it is also the beginning of a new one.

Spiritual author Angeles Arrien put it this way, "The second half of life is the ultimate initiation. In it, we encounter those new, unexpected, unfamiliar, and unknowable moments that remind us that we are a sacred mystery made manifest. If we truly understand what is required of us at this stage, we are blessed with an enormous opportunity to develop and embody wisdom and character."

To understand this secret, we need to look at the nature of

initiation. In its simplest form, initiation means being moved from one state or stage of life to another. Indigenous cultures understood this better than we do and created rituals to place it in a sacred context, like rites of passage. Retirement and birthday parties fail as initiations so life itself initiates us through the many shocks of aging, like the ending of your work life, changing health and physical vitality, the death of a friend or spouse, a diagnosis of cancer or drop in income. But the point is this: whatever changes your life, whatever ends your old life and pushes you into a new one, is your initiation. It can be medical, economic, social or emotional; it can be a big event or an accumulation of little ones that push you over the tipping point – but you know without a doubt that your life has been forever changed. Huge questions rise up inside: "Who am I now?" "What do I do with myself?" "What is this time for?" "How will I face my future, including decline and death?" Nothing seems familiar. But here's the magic: if you pay attention, you will also discover that an unexpected adventure in consciousness has already begun.

On the other hand, if you don't recognize these changes as initiation, you'll miss their power and importance in your life, hang onto the same old identity, and go on doing an imitation of your old self. It won't bring you happiness or fulfillment. Aging represents the defeat of the ego and birth of the soul. It's the death-and-rebirth archetype all over again. It's that big!

Reflections

Here are some questions for older readers to journal on and younger readers to anticipate:

- Can you identify when and how you got initiated? What happened?
- How did you feel about leaving the middle years and crossing over into a new time?

- How has this first secret affected your life?
- Do you sense something really big is beginning to happen to you? What do you imagine it is?

Secret II. *Aging Is a Transformation of Self and Consciousness.* The secret says that aging is enlightenment in slow motion. It begins spontaneously, naturally and subtly. As we wake up from the illusions of mind, we transition from personal identity to the consciousness of divinity, giving birth to the enlightened elder.

This is huge. If this doesn't get your attention, I don't know what will. This goes way beyond conventional aging and yet it is one of the potential gifts of our new longevity. Secret II says that "you" and the identity you've had all your whole life can disappear. How can that happen and what do we experience? Here are the transitional steps that make this transformation possible.

To begin with, I think it's pretty obvious that much of the "you" you used to be is disappearing or long gone. Is your body the same as it was in the middle years? How about your appearance? Do you still play the same social roles – parent, worker, householder – or have the same identity that you had during the career and family years? Instead of all that, now you wear this funny disguise of an aged person. Look in the mirror: there is almost nothing left of the old you! If that's not transformation, I don't know what is! But all this is only the beginning.

This disappearance of the old self – body, appearance, career, and identity – is part of the emptying of aging. It's like tacking a jigsaw puzzle picture of your life on the wall and then watching the pieces begin to fall off. (Spoiler Alert: God shines through the open spaces; but we'll get to that later.) And this dissolution of the old self marks the beginning of the great and central archetype of aging: death and rebirth, which is also the central archetype for enlightenment – isn't that interesting! This surrender of the old "you" is what the mystics have talked about for eons as the prerequisite for enlightenment. It happens naturally in aging.

What's the alternative to the continuing charade of the old you? The first answer involves the continuing evolution of the true self – who we really are inside, who you were born to be, your most natural self. It keeps blossoming like a flower, especially now that the performance pressures of the persona are rapidly fading. Individuation does not stop in aging, it continues. And this is wonderful – new interests, emerging talents, creative self-expression – all sorts of things can happen. This is the psychological dimension of this rebirth – the authentic self, finally free from the responsibilities and goals of the middle years, can grow anew. My older friends are doing the most amazing things these days that I would never have expected! They have come alive in new ways!

A second path takes us into the spiritual-mystical dimension of this transformational time. Since most of what we used to be is now just thought and memory, what would happen if we momentarily stopped thinking and reciting the story of "me" and examined what is left? What is it that remains when thinking ceases? The answer is consciousness. It's always here, and if you focus increasingly on consciousness, something shifts. You no longer believe and identify with your thoughts. They are just thoughts. You are not what you think! Who are you? You are the consciousness in which thought arises.

Here is where aging becomes a mystical experience. As we learned in Chapter 5, we discover that consciousness is not just in me, I am in it, and it is the consciousness of the divine. Ageless, timeless, eternal, and pure, transformative – this is consciousness. And more to the point, this consciousness is God. To be conscious of consciousness itself is to experience God directly. Consciousness is your opening to the divine self. In sum, this is the path that transforms the enlightened elder into the divine human! This reorientation is like Galileo proclaiming that the sun, not the Earth, is the center of the universe. Now the ego is no longer the center of the personality, divine consciousness is.

A Short Quiz on Your Awakening

To ground this conversation, let's look more closely at this experience of changing consciousness. I'm going to describe some of the changes in consciousness older readers might already be experiencing, the changes that come with this subtle enlightenment process. For those over 60, see which changes you recognize and keep a tally.

So, have you noticed...

1. A gradual fading of identity, as if who you were or think you are is no longer very important or even that real.

2. The progressive dissolution of time's importance in your life, so that clock, day planner, and calendar no longer drive your day, and the distinctions of past, present, and future seem less real or important. I sometimes can't remember what day or month it is! You still have a day planner, but it's not the tyrant it was.

3. A loss of "high gear," that hard-driving, goal-oriented focus on getting things done, and a concomitant shift in values from pressured doing to naturally flowing being.

4. Loss of interest in and attachment to material things that once seemed important. Stuff! Now it's clutter, you don't want so much of it.

5. Memory failures for names, dates, details, information, intentions, ideas, and habits that may initially trigger concerns about senility but instead reflect a letting go of

information that is no longer important or meaningful.

6. Moments of silence, stillness, and timelessness, when it seems as if the mystery of eternity were leaking into your everyday world, moments with time stops. For example, sitting in your kitchen, sipping tea, watching dust motes dance in the sun stream through the shutters, you lose track of time and everything else.

7. An awareness of a larger consciousness existing all around you, filling all space and time, and feeling a sense of comfort, peace, and reassurance of its "Presence."

8. Spontaneous spiritual insights that surprise you with their depth and significance. In other words, things you had to think about before but now you just know.

9. Increasing awareness of the sensory richness of everyday life discovered with a still and empty mind, and an increasing enjoyment of living in the present, sensing every moment as precious just as it is.

10. Moments of unexplained and unconditional joy, childlike innocence, and spontaneous playfulness.

11. A loss of personal boundaries, when it feels as if you are what you're looking at, allowing you to feel one with a friend, a plant, the Earth, or even the whole Cosmos, and know the world as Self.

12. A spontaneous welling up of gratitude, concern, and love for the whole world and its peoples, animals, plants, insects, cycles and processes.

Now add up the number of subtle changes you noticed in yourself.

If you're old enough, you've probably experienced many of them though you may not have paid attention or you blamed them on "senior moments." But how would you feel if these changes were signs of enlightenment? We're changing the frame here – aging is not about decline, it's about awakening! Here's the moral of Secret II. When the mind's obsessive thinking ceases, what's left is God's consciousness. And, experiencing your own consciousness as divine consciousness will progressively change you.

Secret III. *Aging is a Revelation of Heaven on Earth.* As the veil of thought dissolves in conscious aging, Heaven on Earth begins to shine everywhere and the world is sacred once again. We have come home from our long journey through the world of thought and invite others to join us in a new consciousness of Creation. Surprise! Aging is itself a mystical experience that naturally reveals the divine world described in Chapter 6.

Now you can view this secret from psychological, spiritual or mystical perspectives. The psychological portion reflects the growth of a bright new life following the rebirth of your true self: new interests, friends, and creative expression – a psychological Heaven on Earth. But as we have seen, this secret also involves a *mystical* shift, a new state of consciousness. As consciousness clears of thought and self-preoccupation, as we move from *conceiving* the environment with thought to *perceiving* it in sensory wonder, the world becomes ever more magical. If we age consciously, Heaven becomes our real and direct awareness of Earth, for the veil of thought and belief no longer obscures it. Why is this important? If we all knew who and where we really were, as Secrets II and III reveal, everything would change. This is one of the great spiritual and mystical tasks of the New Aging.

Four Questions to Guide Your Aging

I want to offer one more tool to use in your aging experience. It consists of four open-ended questions for journal writing meant to help you understand the unique psychological and spiritual tasks of your own aging. Take your time. Go deep. Generate as many answers as you can to each question and don't censor yourself. When you're done, review your responses, underline the ones that speak most directly to your heart, and reflect on what you've learned. If you spend enough time with these questions, you will be surprised at how deep you will go and what they will reveal. These questions will also prepare you to discover the divine gifts and purposes that brought you here.

- Have I accomplished anything with my life? If so, what?
- Why am I still here?
- How do I prepare to die?
- What is love?

I believe conscious elders are participating directly in a new stage in human spiritual evolution amidst the world's shocking and dangerous upheaval. Will we simply retreat to our memories, repeat the past, do what we've always done, or express something genuinely new – new blossoms of the true and mystical selves to help transform our corrupt and fragmented society? With our unprecedented longevity and inspired awakening, elders can integrate a lifetime of wisdom into the experience of the divine human to serve the world anew. Mystical activism is a perfect fit for enlightened elders, renewing our capacity for purpose, love and service.

Aging or not, you will soon explore your divine path in Part III. In the meantime, we turn to the mystical themes found in myth and fairy tale for more universal insights into humanity's collective transformation.

Chapter 9

Mysticism in Myth and Fairy Tale: Three Stories to Awaken Consciousness

Mysticism has been around since the dawn of time so it's not surprising we see its teachings scattered in myths, fairy tales, fables and parables. Here are three mystical teaching stories taken from the world's vast library. In the ancient language of symbol and metaphor, they speak of our ultimate reasons for coming into the world, our responsibility in creating the illusions we suffer, and our work as divine humans. These stories are powerful in their insights and pleasurable in their entertainment. I offer them as respite, reward and refresher after our long and challenging journey through the lands of the religious psyche.

Why Coyotes Bay at the Moon – Finding the Gifts of the True Self

This myth comes from the Pueblo Indians living near Santa Fe, New Mexico. True to the oral tradition, I heard it from a friend many years ago.

Soon after the Great Spirit made this world, he was sitting alone one night gazing up into the dark and empty sky, which contained no moon, stars or light of any kind. He saw nothing but pitch-black nothingness. After a long while, the Great Spirit looked for Po-Say-Wa, the coyote, whose name means "one who hangs his head."

Po-Say-Wa quickly responded – you don't ignore the Great Spirit. The Great Spirit presented him with a large leather bag tied tightly with sinew, and said, "You must take this bag, and follow the trail that winds through the mountains and deserts. Open the bag only when you get to the end of the journey, not before. Your travels may be long and hard, but you are not to stop until you reach your destination."

The fact that the Great Spirit had picked him for such a great assignment surprised Po-Say-Wa. He was, after all, not highly regarded by the other creatures of the world. Perhaps it was because he sneaked around scavenging for food and taking anything he could find – sometimes even taking it from others. Thrilled by this great honor, Po-Say-Wa began his journey – head up, feeling important and determined.

Days and nights, nights and days, Po-Say-Wa journeyed onward, and the trail was indeed long and hard. He crossed steep rocky cliffs, dry and barren deserts. As time went by, Po-Say-Wa began to lose both his sense of pride and his resolve. One evening, as the sky grew dark and hunger crowded out ambition, Po-Say-Wa began to chew absent-mindedly on the sinew securing the bag. It was delicious! Hungry for more, he kept on chewing. As darkness fell, he realized he had eaten all the sinew.

Suddenly, the leather bag burst open. "Oh what have I done?" he cried. Then, to Po-Say-Wa's astonishment, out from the bag flew clouds of glittering mica. Just as quickly, the mica's glowing flakes floated into the night sky, spreading out to become a canopy of sparkling stars. And then a huge ball of mica rose from the bag, taking its place in the sky as the moon. "Oh, my God," whispered Po-Say-Wa in awe and fear.

As Po-Say-Wa looked up at the sky, he only could think of how he had failed the Great Spirit by opening the bag before reaching the trail's end. The night grew cold, and Po-Say-Wa shivered in despair. Finally, full of shame and disappointment, he raised his head and let out a sorrowful cry to the on-looking heavens. The Pueblo Indians say this is why coyotes walk with their tails dragging and heads hung low. When they see the moon gazing down on them with its accusing look, they cry out in shame and sorrow.

Interpretation

This story suggests that divinity entrusts each of us, no matter how lowly or unimportant, with something precious to deliver on our long and winding journey through life. It tells us that somehow, even in our most abject failures, we give birth to the divine and fill the world with its beauty.

Like Po-Say-Wa, we each carry the precious treasure of the true self entrusted to us by the Great Spirit and filled with the gifts we are meant to bring into the world. And, like Po-Say-Wa, we, too, become distracted by the ego's self-idea and grandiose fantasies, and spend years pridefully posturing in the World of Man. Eventually, however, we grow weary of carrying this burden of the false self and start gnawing to get at what's really inside. To get at this hidden treasure, our grand outer mission in the World of Man must fail so we can search inside the "bag" of Darkness within ourselves. The miracle, of course, comes next. In opening the medicine bag of our soul, we release our divinity to the world, thus contributing to the beauty of Heaven on Earth that we all are meant to share.

Sadly, the defeat of the false self in the World of Man often makes us believe that we have failed. Po-Say-Wa represents that part of us that doesn't yet comprehend and celebrate the value of dismantling the inflated self-concept or realize how this allows us to express our true self instead. If he could relinquish the negative beliefs that caused him to sink into the painful Darkness in the first place, Po-Say-Wa would realize the glorious role he played in the building of Heaven on Earth. If we followed suit, we might do the same.

Fetch Me a Cup of Water – The Power of Enchantment

This second story, which comes from the Eastern tradition, can be found in both Hindu and Buddhist variations, and places the responsibility for the many illusions we create squarely in our own minds.

Narada, whose name means wisdom giver, was a famous devotee of the god Vishnu. He journeyed to visit Lord Krishna to ask him to explain Maya, the cause of the world's illusions.

While out for a walk, Narada said to Lord Krishna, "The great sages tell of Maya, the power by which you make the whole universe appear to be what it is not, deluding us into ideas of you and me, this and that, now and then, and the multiplicity of things, when all is one unity. What is this power of Maya? Will you reveal its secrets to me?"

"I will happily fulfill your desire," Krishna replied as they continued their stroll. After walking a very long distance, Krishna became quite thirsty, and said, "Narada, I am thirsty. We cannot return home to quench my thirst. Can you get me a cup of water from the village up ahead? I will sit here until you return."

"Your wish is my command, Lord Krishna."

Filled with the desire to be of service to this incarnation of Vishnu, Narada hurried on to the village. He reached the first house and knocked on the door, which was opened by a young girl whose radiant beauty immediately enchanted him. Instantly he forgot all about Krishna and his request for water and instead fell head over heels in love. Narada asked, "Who are you and who is your father? I would be most fortunate and blessed if I might marry you."

"My father is inside. Come in," she said, whereupon Narada met and discussed marriage with the young woman's father.

"Sir, my name is Narada. I am Krishna's devoted servant. I have fallen in love with your daughter and wish to marry her. It would be the grace of Brahman if you consented." Her father readily accepted Narada's proposal.

The wedding took place in a matter of days. Over the next twelve years, Narada's wife bore him several children and great happiness filled his family life.

One day, however, the sky grew unusually dark, rain clouds mounted, the winds howled furiously and thunderclaps shook the landscape. Soon the village was flooded and many ran to escape the rising waters. Narada collected his most precious belongings, held

*hands with his wife and children, carried the youngest children
on his shoulders, and waded into the swift current. The swirling
waters soon took all his belongings and he cried out for his lost
wealth. The waters then took his beloved oldest son and then, one
by one, the rest of his children. Narada's suffering grew nearly
unbearable. He clung desperately to his wife and cried out, "Why
have you forsaken me, Krishna? Why do you not protect your
faithful servant?" Suddenly a huge wave tore his wife from him. In
that moment, life became hopeless and meaningless.*

*As if in response to Narada's final anguished cry, an immense
flash of lightning lit up the dark sky momentarily blinding his eyes.
When he opened them again, he was stunned by what lay before
him. Or more correctly, what didn't. The storm, the devastation, his
family, and the village were utterly and completely gone, replaced
by the visage of Krishna, sitting quietly beneath a tree, looking at
him.*

*"Narada, I have been awaiting your return for almost half an
hour. Have you brought me the water I requested?" A mischievous
smile began to play on Krishna's face.*

*Suddenly Narada understood everything. He rushed to Krishna,
bowed low, and wept like a child. "Today," Narada said, "you showed
me the power of Maya and I was completely deluded. The Maya of
self, family and everyday life made me confuse the impermanent
world of desire with the joy and release of transcendence. Pursuing
illusions, I lost you and wandered instead in a delirium of fantasy.
Please, Krishna, may I never be so affected again."*

*Without hesitation, and filled with love, Krishna granted
Narada's wish and touched him gently, whereupon Narada found
himself in the highest realms of Heaven.*

Interpretation

Maya, a Sanskrit word, is a central idea in Eastern religious
traditions. The root *ma* means "not" and *ya* translates loosely
to "that." This definition is meant to imply that things are not

what they seem. Rather, the mind, with its constant thought, imagination, and fantasy, colors and distorts all we see, projecting its images onto reality like a movie film. In this way, Maya creates the illusions that drive our busy and often distressing world.

Narada asks Krishna how Maya functions, and his request is granted sooner and more powerfully than he ever expected. He was shown how quickly and easily his consciousness could be completely hijacked by the illusions of fantasy – literally instantly! – illusions that held him in a dream-like state for years. Like us, all it takes is a pretty girl, new ambition, critical remark, or worried thought, and our thought-free consciousness is taken over by an imagined emotional drama. It's not that events don't happen, it's not that love, marriage, children and career are wrong, it's that we project so much additional meaning onto them – fantasies of fulfillment, feelings of inferiority, fears of failure or dreams of fame.

When we learn to examine the World of Man in a consciousness free of thought and fantasy, we discover that it is not what we imagine. Some argue that our whole life is a dream manufactured and projected from inside – the light of divinity passing through an archetypal film of universal ideas, images and symbols to create the movie of our lives. Whether you believe this or not, it is enough to observe how much of everyday life does in fact conform to this process. As we project soap opera fantasies onto reality – "Does he love me?" "Will I be famous?" "Am I in trouble?" – we create perpetual drama. What would it mean to wake up from this dream? As the story suggests, the path of awakening would lead directly to Heaven, and, as we know now, Heaven need not only be in the next world, for we may also find it here.

The Rabbi's Gift

Our third story, learned from Scott Peck, reminds us that divine consciousness can change the world all by itself. It is retold here in my own words.

A monastery was suffering serious decline. There were only five monks left in the decaying mother house: the abbot and four others, all over seventy. As anyone could see, the order was dying.

One day, as the abbot grieved the ending of his order, he decided to ask a wise old rabbi staying nearby for advice on how to save his monastery. But the old rabbi had nothing to offer, saying only, "It is indeed sad. The people in the village have lost interest in the spirit." After sharing their tears, the abbot asked again on leaving, "Is there no hope, no words you can offer to save my monastery?" "No," said the rabbi, "there is nothing I can say. But there is one thing you should know. One of you at the monastery is the Messiah."

Confused and more than a little dejected, the abbot returned to the monastery. His fellow monks rushed up to ask what the old rabbi had advised. The weary old abbot lamented sadly, "There was nothing he could offer. We had tea, visited, wept, and read the Torah. He did say one peculiar thing on my way out. He said that one of us was the Messiah. I have no idea what he meant."

As winter slowly gave way to spring, the old monks puzzled over the rabbi's strange words. "What did he mean?" "How could the Messiah be one of us?" "And who could it be?" Curiously, reflecting on this strange conundrum brought a change to the monastery. Considering that one of them might actually be the Messiah, the old monks began to treat each other with extraordinary respect and reverence. And in case a monk himself might be the one, each began to treat himself with extraordinary respect and reverence.

Now people from the village still visited the monastery on sunny days to picnic or enjoy its lovely paths. But now, as they visited, they sensed something new and different, something holy, radiating from the five old monks and spreading through the chapel and grounds. Touched by this new ambiance, villagers began returning to the monastery bringing their family and friends. Young men even inquired about joining the order. Soon the monastery filled with new life and energy, and thanks to the rabbi's strange revelation, blossomed again as a center of spiritual learning and illumination. And that's the story of the Rabbi's Gift.

Interpretation

What happened here? Was this transformation of the monastery simply a product of good behavior or respectful attitudes? Or could it be that the idea of being the Messiah began to work inside each monk? Maybe the rabbi's hint actually led to an awakening of divinity, of Christ Consciousness, in the monks. Perhaps the more they focused on it, the more it happened. And as their consciousness changed, so too did the world around them seem to awaken with the radiance of divinity.

These three stories symbolize the goal of life in three ways: 1. discovering, often through hardship, the divine gifts we have come into the world to share; 2. recognizing that this journey of life, while seemingly real and convincing, is profoundly colored by our projections from which we will one day awaken; and 3. discovering our inborn divinity, the divine world, and our work in Creation as we come to understand who we really are. To deepen your insight, put yourself in each story and ask how it might symbolize a chapter from your own life.

As Heaven's Compass suggests, we are born into Creation, replace it with a world of thoughts and illusions, and gradually see through them to discover that the divine is the world and so are we. This discovery, in a nutshell, is the essence of mystical activism: we dissolve the illusions of the World of Man, discover Heaven on Earth underneath, see the beauty everywhere, and then share this awakening and our divine gifts with a world still lost in thought. How we do this comes next.

Part III

Mystical Activism: Transforming the World of Man

Chapter 10

Mystical Activism: Heaven's Compass and the Power of Consciousness

In the experience of mystical consciousness, we see through the illusions created by the World of Man and naturally begin to wake up and help each other and the world. All we do from this amazing consciousness is, in effect, mystical activism.

The Great Work

Visionaries of our time, including Thomas Berry, Joanna Macy, and Matthew Fox, describe our collective human crisis as the greatest modern threat of our species. But Fox, who has been one of my own mentors, also offers hope, explaining, "Cosmology teaches us that there is only one work going on in the universe, the 'Great Work' of creation itself – the work of creation unfolding." I believe this Great Work unfolds through us! When we wake up to who and where we really are, and express the divine aliveness of our true self, we join this work and become it. In other words, The Great Work arises from the depths of our own being and we are moved by divinity to participate in its sacred cosmogenesis. And now more than ever we need to be involved in this work.

Heaven's Compass suggests that change doesn't come easily from inside the World of Man. Challenges to World of Man beliefs and principles typically provoke equal and opposite arguments in return. It's warring narratives. Yes, voting helps, lawsuits help, demonstrations help, and standing up to injustice helps, and some change is happening, albeit slowly, but the pendulum still swings back and forth because politics is a projection of the human psyche, and the psyche hasn't changed for millennia! In my lifetime, I've seen more than a dozen presidential administrations and where are we now? We see progress in technology, medicine, and science, but in the maturity of human political discourse, not so much. Instead, we create stereotypical stories about each other, defend these stories, and use them to maintain the endless cycles of conflict, violence and blame. Arguments won't bring peace; only peace brings peace, and waking up from our illusions is the beginning of real peace. It is also the beginning of mystical activism.

What Is Activism?

Activism in general may be broadly defined as efforts to promote social, political, and environmental progress to remediate the suffering of humans and other life forms. These efforts include *social activism, sacred activism,* and *the mystical activism of self-transformation.* Because activism is not a "one size fits all" process, we must each find the path best suited to our own values, nature, personal wounding, and life experience. In fact, we may use more than one type of activism in our helping efforts.

In social activism, our deep beliefs and values inspire us to stand up to injustice and suffering through social, political and legal campaigns, organized marches and demonstrations, volunteering, and letter writing and phone calls to our elected politicians. Our activism may be performed individually or through countless organizations ready to put our energy and experience to good use. In social activism, we work within the World of Man to change the World of Man.

In sacred activism, religious commitments, spiritual beliefs and mystical experiences deepen and drive our work in the service of humanity and life on Earth. Blending social movements with spirituality and religion, we fuse psychological, social, political, and sacred dimensions to transform the World of Man. Andrew Harvey's book, *The Hope: A Guide to Sacred Activism,* James O'Dea's book, *The Conscious Activist: Where Activism Meets Mysticism,* and the *Order of the Sacred Earth,* edited by Matthew Fox, Skylar Wilson and Jennifer Listug, are excellent examples of impassioned sacred activism. Finally, to the field of sacred activism we may also add the process known as *"Subtle Activism"* pioneered by David Nicol that creates a coherent group energy field capable of transforming social systems near and far.

There is yet a third form of sanctified activism – the mystical activism of self-transformation. Emerging naturally from the awakened states experienced in sacred activism, it focuses primarily on the radical now of mystical consciousness and the resulting revelation of Creation. We work first on our self, dissolving the personal self-idea into the thought-free consciousness of the mystic, as the monks did in the last chapter. In this awakened state, we move rapidly into a world that is literally sacred and beyond the chains of identity and beliefs. We enter the flow of divine consciousness and being, caring for the sacred world right where we are, and, like Coyote, releasing the gifts of true self and soul to others. We become divine humans in a divine world, our transcendent consciousness transforming the World of Man into Heaven on Earth, and lifting another veil of Maya from our progressive awakening.

The Mystical Activism of Self-Transformation

Since we create the World of Man through our thought processes, transcending a thought-dominated consciousness literally erases this mentally created world, first at the individual level – a tremendously rewarding experience, and then for society as more people learn to perceive Heaven on Earth directly. We might even call this "ontological activism" for we are changing our actual experience of being and producing a synergistic awakening of the collective consciousness. And the message in mystical activism is this: Don't stay trapped in your world of ideas! Wake up from the hypnosis by cultural beliefs, stereotypes, memes or other thought forms. Nothing is what you think. See without thought and discover who and where you really are. In the activism of self-transformation, we change the world one awakening at a time.

In the past, people believed that enlightenment was beyond an individual's personal control but it's increasingly apparent that mystical consciousness does in fact open into the same awakened state. This awakening represents the revolutionary possibility of mystical consciousness. And the catastrophic conditions of climate change now demand this blossoming of self-transformational activism. We either radically wake up or stay on the Titanic of humanity's collective illusions, which is going down anyway!

The mystical activism of self-transformation is a here-and-now activism. We transform ourselves not to convince others to believe something or force institutions to change, but to alter our individual and collective experience of consciousness and reality itself. It's about being utterly transformed and, as divine humans, letting life happen spontaneously from within the experience of divine consciousness. Ultimately, we are each responsible for this transformation. We wake up, enter the divine realm, and become God in motion. This is a totally different kind of activism – unpremeditated, unpredictable, unprescribed, and unselfconscious. We become divine humans and live from the flow of conscious sacred being.

Heaven's Compass as Tool of Mystical Activism

Can we use Heaven's Compass to support this transformation of self, life, work and world? The answer, of course, is "yes." Integrating the psychological and mystical dimensions of human experience, Heaven's Compass now becomes a spiritual tool for transforming personal problems, inspiring mystical activism, and awakening collective action.

Heaven's Compass teaches that every problem is a complex fusion of thoughts, beliefs, expectations, attachments, and emotions. The instant we struggle with a problem we are back in the mental world, the World of Man, and the more we struggle, the more stuck we get. Mystical consciousness provides the exit from this seemingly endless labyrinth. The first step is to release our entanglement from the imagined problems and emotions trapping us in the World of Man in the first place – Quadrants 3 and 4 – and then open to the divine mind for radically new solutions – Quadrants 1 and 2.

Before we begin, I should say a little about the *dialogue* process you will be using. The split-brain structure naturally and beautifully lends itself to spontaneous dialogue between the ego of the left hemisphere – the "I" or "me" talking about "my" problems, and the divine consciousness of the right hemisphere – the Self and countless other spiritual entities. In this process, you, as ego, ask the questions or pose the problem, and ask the specific "other" to respond. At first this process may seem a little artificial or contrived, but once it gets started, you will be amazed at what spontaneously emerges. You can tell the divine "other" is responding because it says things that surprise you, things you didn't expect, things that change your whole perspective on the problem.

Here are three experiential exercises using Heaven's Compass for *personal transformation, individual activism,* and *collective action.* Return to these exercises over and over. You are activating a process of divine revelation.

Personal Transformation with Heaven's Compass: Dialoguing with Divine Presence

Select a problem that is personally important to you and use Heaven's Compass to find new solutions or shift your perspective. All you need to start is a blank piece of paper and a pencil or pen.

1. Begin by slowly drawing the intersecting lines of Heaven's Compass on the sheet of paper. Number and label each quadrant as depicted in Chapter 4. Notice the

centering effect of this act, and spend a moment staring at the matrix to focus your awareness. Reflect on the four realms of consciousness represented by these quadrants. Then, at the top of the page, write the title of the problem you picked to work on. You will not be sharing this exercise with anyone so be as open and honest as possible.

2. Describe the problem in Quadrant 3, the World of Man, by writing down all your thoughts and beliefs about it, saving your feelings for the next quadrant. Take as much time as you need.

3. Next, describe your feelings and emotions associated with the problem in Quadrant 4, Darkness. In other words, get in touch with the feelings triggered by your thoughts. Don't rush this part; feelings come into consciousness at their own pace. You may be surprised by the content or depth of your feelings. You may also use metaphors, images, dreams, or physical sensations that somehow express your feelings. Don't move on until you have truly expressed your feelings as clearly as you can.

4. Now become quiet and still for a few moments. Notice the natural rhythm of your breath. Now move slowly through the Keys to Mystical Consciousness. Be sure to experience each Key fully before moving onto the next. Here are the keys:

Stop Thinking: Stop thinking and writing, and sit quietly in silence and stillness. Every time your thoughts resume, simply remind yourself, "Stop Thinking!"

Heighten Awareness: In the resulting stillness, heighten

and sharpen your senses. Become as alert and awake as you possibly can and add the awakened state of awe.

Experience the World Exactly As It Is: Focus this intensified sensory awareness on the world around you, perceiving your environment exactly as it is, without thought, labels or interpretations. Carefully examine the texture, color and pattern of your skin, clothes or anything nearby. Pure perception without cognition.

Come Into Presence: While still focusing on a specific perception (e.g., your hand or clothing), become intensely conscious of consciousness itself. Then see if you sense a living consciousness all around you, filling the stillness and silence of space. Sense this consciousness as divinity, because it is.

To focus and intensify your experience of Presence, whisper its name (whatever name feels comfortable to you) and notice what changes in your consciousness, feelings, sensory awareness, or surroundings. Try to sense the experiential qualities associated with this Presence, including unconditional love, warmth, patience and kindness. Be aware of the feelings that tell you Presence is near, including spontaneous joy, relief, gratitude, and peace. Stay in the Presence, and let the experience deepen.

5.   Begin writing a dialogue with the Presence in Quadrant 1, Divinity. Indicate who is speaking by using your initials and "P" for Presence (or a letter denoting a name you prefer). Begin by greeting Presence as you would a beloved friend and describing how it feels to be together again. Then silently write about your problem. Say

what's in your heart, how you feel and what you need. Let the dialogue become spontaneous and interactive. Trust what comes into consciousness. A real dialogue will be animated, alive and often surprising. Be sure God's responses are coming from the experience of Presence and not from a predetermined point of view, which will feel like an increasingly boring or frustrating conversation with yourself. If your dialogue bogs down in repetitive or abstract ideas, you have lost contact with the Presence. Stop the dialogue, repeat the Keys, and wait for the interaction to feel more real. Be sure to record the dialogue's flow and what Presence communicates to you. Stop the dialogue when it feels satisfying or complete.

6. Now begin to move into Quadrant 2, the experience of Heaven on Earth, and complete the following two instructions:

Still acutely aware of Presence, vividly experience the physical environment around you exactly as it is. Do this slowly, deliberately, intently. In other words, see – really see – the colors, textures, patterns, and quality of light in the world, and notice the radiant beauty of things, plants, people, and architecture. Hear – really hear – the sounds of nature, people, things, even silence. Touch – really touch – your own body, clothes, the chair, floor, or walls, and feel the tactile sensations of pressure, texture and temperature as well as the movement of air in the room. Smell – really smell – the fragrances around you, and see how many you notice. Move around slowly to sense – really sense – your body, its grace, weight, and physical sensations – and experience this physical ground of divine Being. And all through this process, repeat the Stop Thinking Key whenever you drift into worry, criticism, analysis, or comparisons. Stay with naked perception until you discover a pristine world cleansed of distorting ideas and beliefs.

Next, to further stimulate the perception of Heaven on Earth, repeat the phrase, "If this were Heaven on Earth, then..." and write whatever you notice, feel or realize. You may also elect to continue your dialogue with Presence here to further sharpen your understanding and perception of the divine world. Record your observations and dialogue in the quadrant labeled "Heaven on Earth."

7. Now that you have filled in all four quadrants, sit back and review the matrix as a whole. Ask yourself: How do my responses differ in each quadrant? What can I learn from these differences? How has my experience of the problem changed? What new insights have arisen? How does this exercise make me feel? Summarize your discoveries on the back of the paper.

8. When the process feels complete, move around a little, regain your normal state of mind, and return to your everyday life.

Two more thoughts. In the process of working on a personal problem, it may change or take on new forms. Sometimes a problem needs to be worked on several times to transcend its hold on you. Secondly, as you become more proficient with Heaven's Compass, these steps will flow more easily and the process will become internalized and spontaneous.

Individual Mystical Activism with Heaven's Compass

Heaven's Compass can also inspire new forms of activism in the world. Unlike the pain and anger triggered inside by negative thoughts and comments, generating inspirational ideas instead in Quadrant 3 not only produces excitement, hope, and energy in Quadrant 4, they can be further developed and refined in Quadrants 1 and 2 to yield some amazing new activities. Give this exercise a try for divinely inspired ideas.

1. As before, draw the intersecting lines of Heaven's Compass and label the quadrants.

2. Identify something positive you'd like to accomplish in the World of Man and describe it in Quadrant 3. Include the details of your vision or healing work even if they are still only cursory and undeveloped.

3. Drop down into Quadrant 4 and describe the resulting excitement, hopes or new motivations that are stirred. Let the feelings increase and evolve. See where they lead you. If your idea produces doubt, discouragement, or pessimism, describe your feelings as well.

4. Come into Presence in Quadrant 1. Repeat the process described earlier for doing this and then begin a dialogue with divinity about your idea and excitement, or about the negativity you discovered. Take your time. See where the dialogue goes and be sure to accept any new understandings that arise even if different from your original inspiration. When your ideas evoke positive energy, the dialogue may help you confirm, refine, energize your idea. On the other hand, divine responses may also alert you to problems, risks or negative outcomes you need to consider. Be open to changing, revising or surrendering the plan. If you have been discussing negative feelings, ask the divine for guidance on how to proceed. If you reach an impasse, take a break

or explore it in the personal transformation exercise described earlier.

5. Assuming your plans have evolved positively, move now into Quadrant 2. Visualize the plan growing organically toward wonderful possibilities, including the part you might play in their actualization. Do not get attached to any particular outcomes; instead, trust that seeds planted will grow in the living soil of divine being. Picture Heaven on Earth shining bright with this new activity.

6. Review what you've written, add new insights and observations on the back of the page, and release the inspired possibility to manifest spontaneously in whatever way is natural and best. Because your dialogue with Divinity and exploration of Heaven on Earth are forms of divine revelation, take your discoveries and inspiration seriously. You are on the threshold of enlightened creation. Notice how your activism becomes infused with new and divine insights, energies, vision and motivation. Notice, too, how your reactions to problems and obstacles lessen as you see through the World of Man to real change. Continue transforming your activism into mystical awakening as you find open perception to Heaven on Earth. Sometimes an inspiring project needs to evolve through several stages. Consider repeating this exercise until you feel truly released and inspired by your new insights.

7. Return to your conventional state of consciousness and resume your day's activities.

Using Heaven's Compass for Collective Activism
Heaven's Compass can also facilitate group-focused mystical

activism, offering a powerful new way to create shared vision, energy and purpose. Here are the steps:

1. Convene your group. Be sure to get acquainted and discuss common values before beginning the exercise. Briefly explain the process, draw Heaven's Compass for all to see, and obtain a commitment to give this exercise a try. Collectively define the nature and parameters of the problem without giving opinions. Encourage the group to engage deep listening and avoid interrupting and cross talk throughout the process.

2. Begin in Quadrant 3 by facilitating a discussion of facts, beliefs, opinions, and other thoughts about the presenting problem. List them on a chalk or dry erase board. Be sure every idea is listed without judgment or debate on its veracity or reality.

3. Move into Quadrant 4. Invite people to share their feelings next. Encourage and accept all feelings without judgment and list on the board. Be sure not to rush this process; it needs to be a meaningful and cathartic process.

4. Enter Quadrant 1 by asking everyone to become quiet. Spend time in silence, stillness, or meditation, and then invite Presence into the room, and encourage people to sense it in whatever way feels most natural for them.

5. Ask people to individually begin writing a dialogue to Presence about the problem. Hand out paper and pencils if necessary. Writing continues until everyone feels complete. Then ask people to underline their most important realizations or revelations about the process.

6. One by one, members share those realizations and revelations. Facilitator paraphrases their discoveries and writes them on the board.

7. Facilitator now asks for a conscious, respectful and sacred discussion of the revelations, avoiding cross talk, interruptions or judgments. What common themes have emerged? What really matters here? What is new? This highly inductive and intuitive group process will not only transform the understanding of the problem, it will transform the group. Insights should at first be tentative rather than conclusive, and allow for more creativity to unfold naturally.

8. Ask for a consensus on whether any new conclusions, agreements or plans are now warranted by this experience.

9. The group will sense when it's time to stop. Conclude with thanks and gratitude to all.

10. As mystics, we are natural receivers of divine energies, inspiration, insight and wisdom. Like the group process in Quaker meetings, this exercise taps into our collective depth and asks each of us to be conduits of greater vision, trusting the group's spontaneous revelations without the intrusion of ego, personality or competition.

Extreme Trauma Situations

How do we as mystics respond to extreme or ongoing disasters like earthquakes, tsunamis, wildfires and mass shootings? Here are some additional thoughts.

In an ongoing disaster, our emergency response can alter our consciousness if we pay attention. We may experience extraordinarily clear vision, slow motion time sense, and access to remarkably enhanced physical strength and endurance. We are radically present, acutely focused, and open to the flow of divine guidance and revelation to access our enormous capacity for conscious action in the face of danger. In other words, we spontaneously enter mystical consciousness! Our work is to stay conscious rather than collapse, respond hysterically, or go numb.

If the disaster has ended or quieted down for a moment, we may need to use Heaven's Compass ourselves to process traumatic thoughts (Quadrant 3) and emotions (Quadrant 4), spend time in the deep peace and healing of the divine Presence (Quadrant 1), come home to the world as a sacred place (Quadrant 2). We can do this with or without actually drawing the matrix. Heaven's Compass can also be used to guide supportive listening and counseling of others, focusing first on thoughts and feelings as a cathartic process and then, after the acute emotions have been processed, on the individual's intuitions about the event's spiritual meaning, opportunity for awakening, and positive actions they could take for themselves or others.

The Goalless Goal of Mystical Activism

Mystical Consciousness erases the spell of identity, time and story to reveal instead the infinite beauty and perfection of Creation exactly as it is, including you, me, and everything around us. In this consciousness, we act from an immense, firsthand and life-affirming revelation of sacred being. We realize that we have been the problem all along, for we constantly undermine or refuse our transformation into divine beings. We cling instead to our identities as false selves in a false world. In divine reality on the other hand, we become the love we have always been seeking, and our love can change the world. This transformational work is not about specific long-term goals or heroic enterprises, which often simply reveal the grandiosity of the ego; rather, this kind of activism focuses on doing one thing at a time in a mystically awakened consciousness. No effort, no thought, no goal, no time, no one – just the divine flow. Then, love fills the world here and now, just as it is, wherever we are, and doing happens without a doer.

Mystical activism evolves naturally from mystical consciousness. As we learn to stop thinking and witness the divine world without our usual prejudices, stereotypes and conceptual lenses, our actions begin to flow from mystical consciousness not the ego's self-serving motives. We move through the World of Man now as divine humans, as bodhisattvas, acting from awakened perception and divine love rather than from ignorance and illusion. This does not mean that we give up our current activism; it means that we infuse our work with mystical consciousness. As we allow the Great Work to flow through us, our actions become truly sacred. We remind ourselves that mystical activism is not specifically goal-oriented; rather it flows from our own self-transformation. Whatever work we undertake, we focus on the radical present, stay in the flow of the imminent divine, and let the moment be our guru and guide.

In sum, imagine that you now see the divine world everywhere. Ask yourself, "How differently would I live?" "Would I be more patient and loving, calmer and more trusting?" "Would I experience greater empathy and understanding for the behavior of those still trapped in the mental world of distressing illusions?" "Would I change my way of being an activist?" "How would I be different with plants and animals?" "How would I care for myself?" Our intuitive answers to these kinds of questions reflect the emerging mystical transformation that arises naturally in Heaven on Earth. It is why Heaven's Compass exercises always return there.

Finally, mystical activism is not intended to dismiss the conceptual world of science, medicine and technology, for thought, too, is a divine gift and we need these creations to survive. Instead, mystical self-transformation rebalances the hemispheres, so that right-brain divine inspiration guides left-brain thought and egos get out of the way of scientific progress. In awakened consciousness, the two sides of Heaven's Compass may one day merge into one divine mind, becoming a fertile ground of joy, inspiration and creativity.

There is one more source of activism that we are only just beginning to comprehend. That source is the *soul*.

Chapter 11

From Mystic to Prophet: A New Understanding of Soul

Religious scholars and theologians the world over have offered countless learned treatises on the human soul. Recent discoveries in neuropsychology and mystical consciousness, however, suggest a different understanding of soul. This surprising thesis may completely change the way you look at your soul.

Soul and the Split-Brain

As we discussed earlier, the higher cognitive functions in humans are divided between the two cerebral hemispheres of the brain. The left side deals with speech, language, logic, reasoning, and storytelling – all the processes that we conventionally call mind. The right hemisphere deals with non-conceptual, non-language here-and-now sensory and spatial awareness taking place in largely thought-free consciousness. To present this new theory of soul, we need to delve more deeply into the fascinating history of the split-brain.

In the early 1960s, some people with uncontrolled seizure disorders underwent a neurosurgical procedure to sever the corpus callosum, a thick band of fibers connecting the brain's two cerebral hemispheres. The surgery prevented the seizure from migrating from one hemisphere to the other, mitigating its destructive power. But this surgery also exposed something both unexpected and startling. Sophisticated psychological testing by Sperry and Gazzaniga revealed that when the corpus callosum link was severed, each side of the brain acted independently, with its own cognition, problem-solving strategies, values and desires. Two brains! Two minds! Two autonomous systems of consciousness in the brain. It was astounding. You can still see some of their experiments on YouTube.

The existence of two separate selves, however, raised a very interesting possibility. What if these two selves disagree? Well, in fact, they often do! Here are some examples from actual patients described in the split-brain literature (remember, the left side of the brain controls the right hand and the right side of the brain controls the left hand). A man reaches to hug his wife with his right hand but pushes her away with his left hand. While putting on his necktie to go to work, a man's left hand undoes it so he can't finish. A woman picks out clothes to wear from her closet with her right hand but the left hand keeps reaching for other selections. A right-handed woman takes hours to pack her suitcase for a trip because her left hand keeps taking the clothes out. A subject's left hand is correctly solving a jigsaw puzzle while the right hand keeps interrupting with incorrect solutions. A woman reaches for a cigarette with her right hand but finds the left hand putting it out. A young man was asked what he wanted to do when he graduated from school. His left-brain said, "Draftsman," while the right spelled out "automobile racer." Perhaps the most interesting of all, asked whether he believed in God, a subject's left-brain answered, "No," but the right-brain said, "Yes." In all these examples, the left-brain's ego was trying to direct the show while the right-brain's other "self" had other desires.

After years of studying split-brain patients, Roger Sperry concluded, "Everything we have seen indicates that the surgery has left these people with two separate minds. That is, two separate spheres of consciousness." Take a moment to reflect on this astounding finding. How does it feel? What might it mean? We are about to discover that it means something truly amazing – the answer to the riddle of who we really are, why we are here, and what mystical activism may ultimately involve.

The Split-Brain and Mystical Consciousness

Many have suggested that mystical consciousness resides in the right-brain, but how might this possibility relate to our normal split-brain functioning? The answer is as amazing as the split-brain itself.

Consider Jill Bolte Taylor's book, *My Stroke of Insight*. Jill is a neuroscientist who suffered a severe left hemisphere stroke that shut down her left-brain. What happened next was unbelievable. She described,

> *In the absence of my left hemisphere's analytical judgment, I was completely entranced by feelings of tranquility, safety, blessedness, euphoria, and omniscience... My left hemisphere had been trained to perceive myself as a solid, separate from others. Now, released from that restrictive circuitry, my right hemisphere relished in its attachment to the eternal flow... whereby I exist at one with the universe. It is the seat of my divine mind, the knower, the wise woman... For all those years of my life, I really had been a figment of my own imagination! ... Now I was simply a being of light radiating life into the world.*

Let me remind you, these are the words of a neuroscientist! Rather than discussing brain structures like the amygdala, hippocampus, or frontal cortex, Jill is talking like a mystic! She now realizes that her right hemisphere literally embodies divine consciousness. And it had been there all along.

Jill is not alone in her discovery of the mystical nature of the right hemisphere. Bede Griffiths, a Catholic monk living for half a century in India who wrote extensively on the integration of Eastern and Western mystical traditions, also suffered a left hemisphere stroke late in life. Afterward, he said it felt like a "blow" on the left side of the head propelling his awareness into the right-brain. As a result, the left-brain's rational mind lost its dominance and the right-brain began taking over. He recalled,

"I was very masculine and patriarchal and had been developing the... left-brain all this time. Now the right-brain... came and hit me." He soon began experiencing overwhelming love, which he described as the divine feminine, and said this experience never left him. Another beloved Western guru, Ram Dass, similarly suffered a left hemisphere stroke after which he experienced tremendously increased levels of love and bliss. He says he has moved from ego to "Soul Land," where "the moment is your guru." I believe Jill Bolte Taylor, Bede Griffiths, and Ram Dass are all talking about the right-brain's mystical consciousness.

Keep in mind, of course, that left hemisphere strokes do not often lead to mystical consciousness for reasons too numerous to list here nor do I recommend them as a spiritual practice. But the observations of these three skilled observers, and the split-brain phenomenon itself, fits our Heaven's Compass model quite well and suggest that we may have far more access to mystical experience than we had previously realized.

I believe that the research of Sperry and Gazzaniga accidentally uncovered a major neuroanatomical portal of mystical consciousness. This is not to say that mystical consciousness is located solely in the right-brain, only that, in the right-brain, it is no longer obscured, overwritten or dominated by the left-brain's thoughts, ideas, beliefs, goals, speech, and identity. The incredible corollary of this argument is that mystical consciousness is always present and it is part of the essential nature of this other "me." Who is this other me? I believe this right-brain mystical self is our soul. When I shift my attention from the left-brain's egocentric thought to the right-brain's thought-free awareness, I can connect with the independent consciousness and desires of my soul, which has always been part of my personality.

Meeting the Soul in Dialogue

In the conversations with Presence exercises in Heaven's Compass, we discussed the nature and possibilities of the dialogue process. In this process, the "I" of the left-brain interacts with the mystical "other" of the right-brain to invite new spiritual insights and revelations that would rarely be discovered by the ego alone. And it's clear that the "other" is not limited to the divine but may include other mystical entities – including soul! – for the right-brain is an open door to the realms of the spirit. Whether we understand the dialogue process as an actual meeting with another being or an imagined conversation with an inner figure from our own psyche, what matters most are the insights discovered and how we grow in the process. Starting with imaginary conversations allows us to develop the dialogue skill. But with practice, some begin to experience their dialogues as actual conversations with entities apart from themselves. In either case, it is always wise to decide for yourself what an experience means and how to integrate it in your life.

I discovered the surprising independence of my soul one day when I began a dialogue with it. His intensity, passion, and confrontative remarks completely surprised me. I was reflecting on the left-brain's ego and its desire to solve the problems of life with big achievements, success, fame, wealth or popularity. I suddenly imagined my soul standing before me, arms crossed, shaking his head, and saying, "Do you still want to do that?" He then told me to go outside, dance in the sunlight, and be ecstatic with the world. I asked if this was his approach to life. But he didn't want to talk about approaches. From this point on, I began recording the conversation. He continued, "That's just more head stuff. The head is your prison. There is no map. Anything you impose as a goal is a lens separating you from the divine and causing you to lose the beauty, magic and perfection of the world. It's so beautiful. Go outside! Wherever you stand is flush with divinity pouring through everything like light pouring through colorful cloth producing so much splendor. Why would you go anyplace else?"

I went outside and, while walking beside the forest, recorded this dialogue on my phone. My soul asserted, "It's now, it's here, it's radiant, it's perfect. It's the divine being – don't go back into your head. Really! This dry grass, this bench, this heat, this blackberry bush, this water – it's all you. You are enlightened the moment you open your senses to all this, to everything that is the divine. Stand still and become one with it, become it, just as it is. You are the divine world as much as the divine world is you. Everything here speaks to you in a language of pure sensation. Everything knows you are here and everything experiences you as alien until you stop and join it. When you stand still and become pure silence and wonder, transparent to the beings and energies of what is, then you're home. Don't go anywhere. Don't have a goal. Just wake up."

I asked my soul if he thought I understood. He nodded but fervently added, "Yes, now do it! You're always getting it, you're never it. But you are it. Just experience yourself and your own being as powerfully and intensely as you do the divine world and then there will be no difference and no separation and no problems and no place to go. You are the substance of divinity too. You are the whole. When you become God like this, there is nothing else you have to do. You become the whole and it becomes you, and then you exude creativity and being and unity like the tree, you exude it by standing still and being. You serve the world by simply being what you are."

"Look around you," he added. "You are walking through the divine world, through Paradise, not even noticing that you are standing at the edge of transformation, the edge of the two worlds. The divine world is so full of the growing and the green and the beautiful and the conscious and you're just plugging along in your head. Compulsivity is one of the enemies. You get into your mind and think you have to do something. These new insights are exciting but then you think you have to make something happen when it's already happened. It happened a million years ago, ten billion years ago, but you keep crushing it out with your World of Man beliefs and perceptions and logic and rules and strangled awareness. There is no place to go, you have already found it, you are looking at it, it is this. Stand still, very still, and you become it and all the boundaries disappear, and you are one with it and it is you."

My soul explained, "This is why you often resist being around people too much," he said, "because what you encounter in the human world is layer after layer of rules and beliefs and expectations and agenda – a fortress of thought forms. Why spend time with that? It's a bedlam of separation, of voices, and cries and alarms and assertions and doubts all acting at the same time."

I asked my soul, "What, then, is my work in all this? What does the universe want from me? What am I to be in this matrix of oneness, perfection and beauty? What is the plan?" He replied, "Dissolve back into God and see through all plants, animals, through all eyes. Hear the ringing of joy everywhere, the pealing of sacred bells, the sound of Creation, and know it, dance it, and love from that place. There is no purpose beyond love, gratitude, celebration, wonder and joy at all that already is. Stay in your awakened heart. Let the rest go. You don't even have to do anything. The World of Man is always a dead end. It's the flypaper, the labyrinth, the quicksand, the false self-seduction. Stay with what you learn on this walk. It's all here. Live in the world of God."

Suddenly, in this new soul consciousness, I found myself wanting to confront the whole false illusion of the World of Man, to point out how much suffering and misunderstanding arise from beliefs and identities, and instead draw attention to love and wonder and the divine world. I wanted to tell others, "You live in a mental construct of stress and ignorance. Wake up. See who and where you really are. You are living in your nightmare. The world's problems will not go away until all understand the destructive power of belief and illusion! It is the cause of so much suffering. I don't want to belong to a world of cruel, false and divisive values – the damage to people and all living things is too great."

When the conversation resumed later on, I learned something else from my soul that I didn't expect. I learned how forceful and persuasive he could be, as evidenced in this exchange:

"Soul, where are you?"

"I am here. You can put me in charge anytime."

"Why am I suddenly hesitant? Why am I afraid?"

"You're afraid I will take you to places you fear."

"Where?"

"Everywhere. I would take you into poor areas, into other people's houses. I would change your personality. I would take over your personality. 'You' would be someone else. Why are you afraid of that?"

"I want to stay in my safe, peaceful space, in my house, in my quiet, separated, undisturbed comfortable space where I can explore my inner life. I don't want to go out of my safety zone. I need my peace and quiet. I need quiet space to explore the boundaries and dynamics of self and soul. Why do you want me to go out? What's wrong with who I already am? Why can't you let me be?"

"You asked me what I would do if you gave me control."

"But why do I have to change? I am doing the work of my inner self, my true self. This is what I was born to do. Why do you want me to leave that and do something else? Who are you?"

"I am your higher self. I am what you could be, your future self. You are hiding from your future. You are hiding from me. The real question is why you're not willing to change. I am showing you what you are capable of. While this may be the theme of your next life, you could start now. Sooner or later you have to take the risk of being me."

I sat stunned by these statements and that my soul could be so direct, impatient and evolved. Its difference from my true self was fascinating and little disconcerting. But I continued the conversation, saying...

"But I don't have the strength you do."

"The false self never does, never will. I am your strength. I am the someone else that will change the world. You won't ever change the world so give me the lead in your body and life."

"Wow. I feel the power you are talking about. I feel your energy and strength. I fear, however, it would give out as my older body's energy runs down."

"I am power from another source, the source of Spirit. It has its own pipeline. It's not you. All you have are excuses."

I admitted, "I am afraid because you are so outspoken and seemingly impulsive. It feels like I can barely contain you. I'm afraid to let you take over. You make me want to say and do the most controversial things. You are so powerful! Can I trust you? Do you actually have good judgment or are you just bold and aggressive?"

"That's the energy I bring. I will be bold in activism without regard for the paltry opinions of the naysayers. It doesn't matter what anyone thinks. I have much to do and say."

"That's what scares me. Can we start small and tentatively?"

"It's time to act, John. I am here to act."

"I need to better understand what this change will mean and prepare myself to give myself over to you."

"A big change is coming, a great change in the way your personality works and how you work. I am the one that you have been waiting for all your life. You are letting the genie out of the bottle and he won't go back in. You are at the threshold of the new world."

"I do know an awful lot about spirituality and I do have much to teach and share. Maybe it is time."

"It's time. I will be you. I will inhabit your personality."

"So, our job is to work together on things?"

"Not if you just try to tame me again. You have to give up

control and trust me. I am your greater being, your wisdom, your sacred self. You can't build Heaven on Earth with avoidance, you must assert its reality."

"Whenever I think of you, I feel an expansion of confidence, independence and strength. You fill me with power. I have never had this experience before."

The Movement from Mystic to Prophet

The preceding dialogue revealed something even more powerful – that sometimes the mystic becomes the prophet acting with a newfound inspiration, determination and fearlessness to change the World of Man. One of the first persons to address this shift was theologian William Hocking who wrote in 1912, "... the mystic in action is the prophet. In the prophet, the cognitive certainty of the mystic becomes historic and particular; and this is the necessary destiny of that certainty: mystic experience must complete itself in the prophetic consciousness." But who and what is the prophet?

I believe that the prophet emerges from the mystical consciousness of the right-brain. As the split-brain research revealed, a second consciousness dwells in the right hemisphere inside each of us waiting to be recognized. It emerges as the insistent voice of our soul, an entity completely separate from the ego with its own reasons for being here. Once we learn to quiet the mind and open the connection with the divine world through the dialogue process, soul can step forward borrowing the ego's language facilities to communicate. Not only is much learned, but eventually the soul becomes more assertive, pushing us to risk expressing the gifts of the true self we came into the world to share. The soul transforms into prophet when we use our gifts to challenge, disrupt or awaken the World of Man. Those who follow this mystic-to-soul transition allow soul to act directly in their lives to challenge the World of Man and reveal Heaven on Earth.

The effects of this steady shift from soul to prophet can be subtle, obvious, or even dramatic depending on the gifts we were born to give. Some of us will become fierce and powerful, others may express their gifts through nurturing and caretaking, still others through teaching, art or writing. In this way, the prophet activates the soul's embodiment as true self to transform the world. Mystical activism thus energizes the prophet pouring fierce love into the world.

Meeting Your Soul

It's time now for you to meet your soul. Are you interested? Here is an exercise for exploring what your present and future self wants to say to you. Let it be an imaginary conversation at first and be open to wherever it goes. Here are the instructions for your conversation with soul.

1. Find a comfortable spot to sit and write. Have paper and pen within reach. Be sure your chair is comfortable. Now let your thoughts slow down and unwind. Let your breathing relax into a gentle rhythm. Become peaceful and clear your mind.

2. Imagine that you can shift your attention from left-brain thinking to right-brain awareness. Pure awareness. Let thinking cease and awareness open.

3. Now imagine that you can see your soul somewhere in the room. Take your time. Let his or her image spontaneously come to you. Where is he or she standing or sitting in the room?

4. Let the image become clearer. What does your soul look like? Describe its physical appearance, clothes and age. What is his or her expression, mood, attitude or emotional

energy? Let the image become clearer little by little, as if adjusting the lens on binoculars to bring something into focus.

5. Welcome your soul in whatever way you like. Talk to your soul. How does your soul respond to your reaching out?

6. Get out your paper and pen and prepare to record a dialogue with soul. Write your name and whatever name you wish to use for your soul.

7. Begin the dialogue. You might start by saying how you feel, what's been on your mind, or asking a question. When you've expressed yourself, sense the soul's energy and let your soul respond. Record the response without censoring or judging it. Accept whatever is said and then write your response.

8. Continue in this fashion pursuing any topics that are important to you. Topics can include relationships, work, feelings, struggles, hopes, dreams, spirituality, God, anything. You will know that the dialogue is authentic if your soul responds in ways that surprise, teach or affect you emotionally. The soul's vision almost always provides new information.

9. You may also find your soul being more assertive than you would have expected, as it pushes you to explore your reasons for coming into the world. The prophet archetype of the soul insists on action.

10. If you're ready, let your soul move into you now. Imagine it actually enters your body and that you can feel its

presence, energy and activation. What do you notice? What changes for you? How do you feel with the soul's presence inside you? How do you feel tempted to act? Continue the dialogue.

11. When the dialogue feels complete or runs out of gas, stop and reread it. Then write your reflections on what was revealed. What did you learn? How do you feel? What was your soul's message?

12. Remember that you can invite another dialogue anytime you wish but always be sure the responses are coming from your soul, not your head, and that you're not writing what you already know. Realize also that you as ego still have control. You do not need to be afraid of actually losing control of yourself or your personality.

13. When you're ready, thank your soul for its participation. Restore normal consciousness, let your image of soul fade away, and return to the room as it is.

As you will learn, the soul minces no words and may not be interested in what "you" want or think, that is, what you desire from the ego's perspective. Soul wants awakening, transformation, and action. In this way, the soul can become a guide, cheerleader or insistent voice encouraging and even demanding change so the world will change. Your soul can give you energy or temporarily take over control with your permission. You can also evolve a partnership relation with soul.

This new understanding of soul is revolutionary. The value of this new consciousness, however, is that you can become a leader, inspired, energized, and guided by the higher and future "you." This is yet another kind of mystical activism, one with great power and vision. Make friends with your soul – it's why you came into the world.

There is also more help for our mystical activism on the horizon. We can reach through the veil to the other side and welcome our ancestors, spirit guides, angels, and other spirit beings who long to help us make the soulful changes. They, too, come through the right hemisphere's mystical portal. They remind us we are not alone.

Chapter 12

Help from the Other Side: Reaching Through the Veil

The vertical boundary depicted in Heaven's Compass separating the World of Man from Heaven on Earth is replicated in the division that thought creates between this world and the next or "other" world. This schism is of our own creation, of the mind. It masks the permeability of this veil and the ease with which consciousness can move back and forth across it. As the Near-Death literature suggests, death is an artificial boundary for our consciousness which continues on after the body dies. Similarly, in dreams, departed loved ones often return to us in ways that are more than symbolic. This chapter addresses the nature, reality and possibilities of our connection to the spirit world drawn from my own experiences. I share them to illustrate how readily we can contact the spirit world to heal relationships, support our activism, understand the nature of reality, and grow spiritually. But please read this material with an open mind – the moment we ridicule or dismiss these relationships, that moment we lose touch with them.

Ancestors, Spirit Guides and Angels

Throughout human history and to the present, people from virtually all cultures have believed that ancestors, spirit guides, angels, and other spiritual beings operate here as well as in the next world. They are felt to be deeply interested in our lives and welfare on Earth. Indeed, the classical literature on angels is enormous, positing vastly more angels than humans and arranging them in complex hierarchies that support the entire divine cosmos. Despite the advent of scientific materialism, such beliefs are alive and well. Ancestor connections are honored in prayers, continuing felt relationships, dreams, and cultural celebrations, like All Saints' Day and the Day of the Dead. Indeed, a Gallup poll in 2016 found nearly 90% of those questioned acknowledging a belief in angels, and informal surveys of workshop audiences typically find the majority sharing this belief. These beliefs and experiences suggest that the reality we create in the World of Man is still permeated with intuitions and encounters from the other world.

We can reach out to ancestors, angels, and spirit guides in numerous ways and communication can be direct and indirect. Direct forms include dream encounters, sensing their presence around us, dialogues in mystical consciousness, Near-Death Experiences, psychic channeling, and their actual assistance during crises or emergencies. We experience indirect contact via intrusive thoughts, intuitions or messages that seem completely out of character for us, as if we were being subtly warned about something or pushed to act in new ways by invisible beings.

Contact with deceased ancestors, angels, and spirit guides often begins with active imagination exercises that grow more fascinating and instructive as our dialogue skill evolves. But I believe that these conversations may also involve messages received in mystical consciousness from those we are seeking to reach. The fact that these dialogues nearly always surprise us with new information, unexpected guidance, or important realizations may further affirm the actual existence of these beings. Writing on prophecy, Thomas Aquinas said, "… one is called a prophet because he… sees imaginary visions, and has an understanding of them…" For Aquinas, "imaginary visions" represented divine sources communicating directly to the receiver's mind. In mystical consciousness, therefore, we stand at the intersection of the worlds, for our dialogues with ancestors, angels or spirit guides invite their presence, words and visions to come through the mystical portal of the right-brain.

Ancestors

Let's start with ancestors. How might our ancestors help us and how might they need our help as well? Through dream visitations and dialogues in mystical consciousness, I often find myself communicating with my parents, grandmother, son, and others who have gone before me. Illustrating the use of dreams and dialogue, here are some examples from our continuing relationships.

After presenting an exciting webinar one day, I had this dream: I'm on the landing of our former house in Sacramento. I turn around, and there is my dad. Really! Dressed as he always was – slacks, flannel shirt, sport coat. I am astonished. He starts hugging and kissing me. It's so real I can feel the solidness of his body and smell his scent. I hug him back and kiss him and keep asking, "What are you doing here? Where have you been?" He says he heard about what I had done and, by implication, seems to be saying that he came to show me how proud he was. He visited me once before, years before, to celebrate the publication of my first book, *Death of a Hero, Birth of the Soul*. He then goes into our computer room where my wife is resting, recovering from an acute illness earlier in the year, and they have an animated conversation as well. When he comes out, I repeat my earlier questions, "Where have you been? What have you been doing?" but the dream ends with no more answers.

Reflecting on these dream images, I realize they have been about my father's love for me and his pleasure at my success, and that he came to share his pleasure. In my journal, a couple days later, I start a dialogue with him. My father says,

I came to you because I love you and because of what you did. You made it possible for the two worlds to merge, to come together! And we from the other side are coming back, we are coming home, tearing down the walls between our worlds. I love what you did. Your work shows the world where Heaven is, that it extends to Earth, that it is Earth too. You have made this reunion much more possible. I want to come back to Earth again and see all the people and places I love. We all do. There should be no division. It will all be better when that happens. I love you, John boy. With that webinar, you cracked the wall. You said the unsayable. Your understanding broke into both worlds, and broke into Earth's collective consciousness. Can you see how happy I am, we are, all of us over here. We want to come home. We want the earth to be part of Heaven and it will be if people can open their consciousness and see! We are one. It's only a matter of people changing their seeing and welcoming us back. It's not that we don't like Heaven, it's that we want to be with you and our families in one world. This is the promised divinization of the world. I love you, I love you, I love you. We're coming home and you'll be able to come here, too. It will finally be one place!

I understood then that my father's effusiveness was more than being proud; it was the joy of homecoming. His message has huge implications for sacred activism. I believe all of us, living and "dead," want to make this place sacred, to reconcile spirit and matter, Heaven and Earth, sacred and profane, God and man. While we may not be conscious of this desire, it's part of our longing for unity and we have our ancestors' support. If we can wake up enough, they can come home and help us build a new unified world. It was an enormous spiritual paradigm shift: The ancestors want to come home with all their skills and realizations and love to help us, rejoin us, and initiate the next stage of our common spiritual unfolding: Heaven on Earth. But we must invite them back!

A few weeks later, I have another conversation with my father that soon includes others.

"Dad, I love you for visiting me in that dream. Now I'm

wondering how to ask you to help. How will this work? Dad, are you there?"

"Of course I am, John-boy. I am with you always. I want to come back. Let me help you."

"By doing what?"

"Well, to start with, go up and tell your wife you love her. Never miss a chance to share your love."

"Okay, I just did. That was good. What now?"

"Look around you. See how beautiful the world is. That's the way you lift the veil. Beauty. It's the divine shining through everything. It's that way in Heaven, only more so. Humans shut it down. That's your work here. See beauty. You know the phrase, 'In beauty it's begun.' And love the children. They are young spirits putting on their personalities. And the animals, they have no need of identities or beliefs. They live in beauty when they feel safe."

"Will my recent professional presentations on aging and spirituality be part of this new world? Am I making a difference?"

"You're saying what's real. That's huge. Keep doing it. It takes a long time to sink in."

"Dad, I feel you in this room. I feel you behind me. I feel your presence. It's absolutely wonderful. I am so sorry I have ignored you for so long lost in my own thought-world."

"I'm so glad to be with you. I get to be your father again, and your friend. You can contact me anytime."

I began to wonder, then, about my other close ancestors, the ones I loved so much before they died. I asked, "What about Gamy? (my grandmother). What does she want?"

"Ask her."

"Gamy, are you here? Where have you been? You haven't come to see me since you left. Are you hurt or angry with me that I didn't see you before you died or come to your funeral?"

"A little. You forgot about me."

"I am so sorry. I was so self-preoccupied at that age, so self-centered. Where are you? What are you doing?"

"I've been waiting for someone to remember me, to think about me, to come for me. But now I'm busy with all there is to do here. And with my son. There is so much joy and spiritual growth on this side."

"I am so sorry I ignored you. That must be so hurtful for you. Gamy, will you come back like Dad to help, to come home? You are such a beautiful soul, so gentle and sensitive. Will you help us unite Heaven and Earth?"

"What could I do?"

"Just be yourself and share what you've learned."

"I've learned how important it is to tell people how you feel, to show your love, to really care for others."

"Do you still write poetry?"

"No."

"Will you write poetry again? It was such a rich expression of your soul."

"Yes I will, and I will share it with you."

"I love you, Gamy. I always did and still do. I love you so much. Did you find your son Johnny? What is he doing?"

"He's so busy. He never got to do all he wanted to on Earth so he's been nonstop busy in Heaven. I hardly ever see him. He's kind of wild."

"I feel your presence here with me now. It is gradually becoming stronger. Will you help us?"

"I'll try. I feel better now. Maybe I do have something to offer. I was always so interested in spirituality and now I have some more direct spiritual experience in Heaven. I think I can share that spiritual presence and energy. I can bring that into your world. Maybe it will help dissolve the veil over your eyes and others."

"Thank you, Gamy. Wow. That's so wonderful."

Then my father chimes in, "There are so many of us who want to help. Your world is full of us. You just shut us out with your beliefs, but there is only one world and no real boundaries. The living stop paying attention and we get tired of the falseness of the World of Man, as you call it. We just can't get through to people's walled-off minds to help."

In these ancestor dialogues, I began to see that our relationships with our loved ones don't end with death and that we carry our struggles into the next world. That thought left me a little worried about my mother.

"Mom, where are you?"

"You don't care. You're all mad at me."

"You're hurt, too. I'm so sorry. I'm not mad at you. We were all victims of confused human relationships, you as much as any."

"I don't like to think of myself as a victim."

"Okay, but forgive yourself. Yes, there were hurts. We're all still learning. Will you come back to help us here?"

"What could I do? I made such a mess of things before."

"What do you think?"

"I can see so much that needs changing. Racism. Ageism. Sexism. Poverty."

"Then come back and help us. Don't stay stuck in your hurt. You could do so much."

"Really? You think so?"

"Yes. You always had a vision of change. Use it. Show people how to solve problems."

"Yes, I could do that. Yes, I will help."

"Mom, I feel you now behind me, in this room, opening your presence to me. Thank you. I know we didn't always connect, we were so different, but that's on both of us. We'll both have to grow our understanding of each other. And you did connect with me in key moments, like when you helped me see my future as a psychologist. Thank you for that especially."

"I did do some good. I'm glad for that. Yes, I will come over and help humanity break out of the prison of mind. I was stuck there, too. We even still get stuck there in Heaven, which is why I was hurting. Thoughts can still trap us."

I ended this unexpected other-worldly visit by speaking again to my father. "Dad, you were always my guide. Now you are again. Why were you my guide?"

"Because I saw that you had the kind of awareness that could understand the world. You were the one to serve humanity by erasing the split, to bring back unity consciousness. I need you, too. Now we can work together to make Heaven real here and now."

"Why do you need me?"

"Because you have skills that I don't have. You've got people skills and mystical skills and spiritual perceptivity. You have what I finally got in Heaven. Now we can work together. I have much to show you, too. I went all through Heaven. I saw how Spirit infuses everything, how energy is Spirit consciousness. And we are that. And you have the tools and credibility to bring that into the world's consciousness. And you must."

Before I left this visit, I needed to speak to my son, Adam, who died in a car accident. I miss him so much but love the ways he comes to me in dreams and spontaneous dialogues. "Adam, I want you to come here, too. Are you interested?"

"Hell, yeah! I'd love to come back and help people with their lives, their music, their energy. I didn't know you could come back. I'm pumped. I'm excited. When do I come?"

"Anytime you want. Try to find people who can sense your presence or your energy so they can absorb your positivity. Come see me! I know your presence. I know you. You are my boy. (Big hug.) I feel you now. God it's great to have you back!"

Later I continued one more discussion with my father.

"Dad, can you tell me more about how we bring the ancestors home?"

"By thinking of me and talking with me, you create a space for me to be here with you. You give me a reality inside you, a home. Then I can be in and operate in your world. This is how we come into your world. You make it possible with your awareness of us. Then, as human consciousness advances, you will see us too, all around you, for there is no separation beyond your mental blinders."

I hope this section didn't include too much dialogue for you. I wanted to illustrate the spontaneity, healing and new insights that can happen in these amazing conversations. Who would you like to talk with? Can you imagine having these kinds of conversations with the people you love from the other side? Give yourself permission to restore these relationships, in your imagination or in what you actually experience, and heal the unfinished wounds we all carry.

Spirit Guides

I believe that loving spirits also seek to support, guide and assist us in our Earthly journey. A wonderful website hosted by Peg Abernathy includes many firsthand descriptions of spirit guides encountered during Near-Death Experiences, including her own. She beautifully summarizes,

> ... they are always with us, talking to us through our intuition, through our hearts, minds and feelings. And some people, blessed with the ability to quiet the mind and receive messages and wisdom within that silence, are able to communicate with these wondrous Beings who wait patiently for us to call out. We are always here. Never do we leave and the moment your thoughts turn to the Light, ours will be directed in that path as well. That is why we are here: to Guide you towards this Light, The Knowing of the Light. Our gentle Guidance of your Soul is just that, Guidance. It is you who make the ultimate choice. And that is the Power of Will. You must understand that we are no better than you, that we seek the same Light as you. If a person wishes to directly contact their Spirit

Guides while in the physical body, it can be done.

I have had amazing conversations with two spirit guides. Beginning with a conversation with my father, I commented,

"Dad, I sense two tall thin figures, a man and woman, older, who are here with me. In fact, I sense their presence now. Do you know them? Do you see them? How do I relate to them?"

"They are always around you. They have been so patient waiting for you to turn and see them."

"They are bigger than I imagined. Really big and powerful. This gives me goosebumps. What are their names? 'Fran and Jan' I hear inside my head. Reminds me of the camp counselor Fran from summer camp who was so nice to me. But they seem a little scary, too."

"Talk to them, not me."

"Okay. It's time. I don't know why I have waited so long. Maybe I was afraid. You seem so powerful. Should I be afraid?"

"We would never hurt you. We are here to help you grow and serve and love. We are here to give you our energy, powerful energy to see into the divine. You have always been a mystic, now you really are one."

"I feel your power. The power of love. The power of Spirit. Of God. It's so powerful. How do I use it? How does it use me? What do I do from here?"

"Stand up. Feel me behind you. Feel me entering your being."

Whoa. My breath catches. I feel the wholeness of power coursing through me. "What now?"

"Now we dance!"

And we do. This is the dance I write about at the end of my book, *The Divine Human*. It is rich and sweet and powerful. "What does it mean to really be a mystic?"

"Come out of the closet. Say the truth out loud: 'I am a mystic. I feel the divine force within me. I see the divine world. I am a divine being. We are all divine beings.'"

"You'll have to help me. I'm afraid that so many of my 'normal' friends and family, and the 'normal' world will be judgmental toward me, or feel alienated from me, or feel I have changed too much."

"You are only being what they are going to be one day in the future. You will be helping them see their own reflection."

"That's such a tall order."

"You are 'coming out' in your workshops. Don't be afraid. We will be with you. We will create the mood so people can really hear your message. Your message is right on."

"Are those your real names?"

"You wouldn't be able to pronounce or even remember our real names. Actually, you picked these two names but they work fine for us."

"Will you tell me your names one day?"

"Yes."

"Dad, whew! What now?"

"Your guides have so much power for you. Open to them. They will completely change you into your angelic nature, your higher nature, your realest nature. Listen to them. Trust them. Ask them for guidance. You are entering Heaven as this experience transforms your being and seeing and knowing."

"I'm kind of overwhelmed but glad I've met you, Fran and Jan. Thank you for your endless patience. I've had to fight against my own skepticism, cynicism, and doubt. But what do I have to lose except spiritual growth if I don't open this dimension of consciousness!"

"We are here to guide you. We are always here. You will meet us in person soon. This is the work of aging – opening to the spirit world! Bringing down the veil."

"Wow. I get it. This is the work of the aging mystic as Divine Human. This is my work. Can I cross over as well?"

"Yes. We will take you across when you're ready. We will open all the doors. It's all in you already, the whole map and experience. You've been here many times. But now it's time to bring the worlds together. That, too, is the work of mystical aging."

"What else can you tell me?"

"It's all good, John. All will be well. We bring you all the energy and wisdom you need. All is possible with us. We will carry you when you're tired. You have now entered a new dimension of existence with so much you don't know but will learn. You have a new and amazing experience before you and you will find much to learn and give. Welcome to the inter-world, the one world experience. You have the ability now to explore the nonmaterial worlds of the greater cosmos and explore the vastness of consciousness from which they arise."

"I hardly know where to start!"

"We will guide you to places and experiences that will expand you the fastest."

"What do I need to learn first?"

"That you, in your truest 'causal' body, are already on both sides. You are pure spirit expanding consciousness more every day. You can now see the overlapping worlds."

"This is a new breakthrough for me. A whole new dimension of awakening. How did this even happen?"

"You finally gave us permission to come into your mind. You can thank your father's visit for that. He came first and showed you how you had already opened the door."

"What should I be seeing or realizing right now?"

"That both worlds coexist and that what is here is there, too, in a more perfect and beautiful form. We are like tourist guides to the realms and lands you will discover with us."

"What else should I know?"

"Everything is one! It is only the mind that divides things like a prism. And once the mind is opened, you can see it all!"

"I get the sense that I can see Heaven itself through the veil of this world. It's so beautiful. What about the dark ugly areas of our world?"

"Go look if you want. It's the level of your awakening that reveals the qualities of area you enter."

"What should I be learning from all this!"

"That all coexists and that you determine your growth. Follow the vibrations of your being and your level of consciousness will keep rising."

"All people have this same beautiful consciousness but don't realize it or its potential."

"You are here to change that. Now you are seeing the next stage of your calling."

"Why is it that we can see the other side when we're near death but not the rest of the time?"

"Because when you're near death, you have finally given up your attachment to the Earth world. You release your belief projections. You finally open your spiritual eyes. You see without any thought except for thoughts of loved ones you need at this time, which calls to them. You release the World of Man and see beyond with your other eyes, the eyes of soul consciousness that can see the other world, and your soul, now free of the false self, remembers being here before."

"So, what is my next step?"

"Stay awake and aware of us. We will show you."

I trust that you are as surprised and amazed as I was as these dialogues unfolded. I never expected any of this but I see now how profoundly spirit guides can teach, support, and mentor us. This, too, is part of our unfolding mystical activism.

Angels

How do we dialogue with angels? What angel would I call upon? Some famous one? I imagine now simply sending forth an intention, a call, a wish to meet an angel. Then this reverie begins...

I see light coming through a dense fog. It grows brighter and brighter. A shining figure emerges, a light being, more light than substance, or better yet, light as substance. It floats in space now before me, looking, waiting, patient, kind.

"Thank you for coming, I think. Who are you?"

"You asked for a visit from an angel, I was in the vicinity."

"Wow. I don't know what to say."

"Take your time. There is no time where I come from."

"Okay. Thank you. What is an angel exactly?"

"We are beings of light that hold the universe together, serve certain divine functions, and help God maintain harmonic order."

"Why does God need help and aren't you kind of like God?"

"God doesn't actually need help, this is a gift we choose that celebrates our being in God. We vibrate with the oneness of divinity and light a path for others."

"Why would someone call on you? Do angels help human beings? What are the guardian angels that so many talk about?"

"That is a lower class of angels that look out for humans. I am not that type of angel. There are actually so many classes of angels."

"Maybe that's why I don't know what to ask. It's so complex. Do I have a guardian angel?"

"You already spoke to them. They are your spirit guides."

"Oh, okay. You responded because you heard my mental call. The cosmos is held together by angels? They are everywhere?"

"Yes. We keep things ordered."

"I thought God didn't actually need you."

"That's true but we stand there anyway in service because we feel one with divine creation in doing this. We align with creation and unite with it and then we merge back into the divine."

"I find this puzzling. You do this service but you don't have to and it's not necessary, it just feels good?"

"Yes. You have unity experiences that feel wonderfully right but God's existence doesn't depend on them. You feel drawn into the implicate order like metal shavings from a magnet and feel beautifully united with divinity. We are drawn like moths to flame and like moths we will be eventually consumed."

"What about guardian angels?"

"We were guardian angels once. Like sober AA or NA members, guardian angels are drawn to helping people still addicted to being humans but eventually we outgrow this need and move on."

"Humans are spirits addicted to the illusions composing the World of Man?"

"You could say that, yes."

"Are humans future angels or fallen angels?"

"Both. Fallen angels have forgotten their divinity, future angels have not yet felt divine enough for it to take hold and keep slipping back."

"So what should I take away from this conversation? And thank you by the way for exposing all this to me."

"I hope you better understand the world of angels for you will join us one day. In fact, you will wake up one day and realize you always were. That's why I could hear you so easily – your spiritual essence is pure."

"Thank you. Do you have a name?"

"Blue Angel will do."

"Why blue?"

"It's the color of…"

"I can't finish that sentence. Why?"

"It's beyond your concepts so you have no words for it yet. You will."

Obstacles to Other-Worldly Help

With so much help available to us, why do we ignore it? Four barriers – disbelief, distraction, failure of imagination and fear – block our contact with the other side, maintaining the veil between worlds.

Scientific positivism, the Western philosophy that credible knowledge only arises from logical, objectively verifiable, sensory measurements and explanations, leaves most of us unwilling to consider mystical or non-ordinary experiences. Distracted by compulsive busyness, we rarely enter the quiet, stillness and presence of mystical consciousness that allows other beings to come into our imagination, a tragic failure of imagination. Finally, fear blocks us from contacting ancestors, angels and spirit guides – fear of failing or incorrectly performing the dialogue exercises, looking downright foolish, or uncovering the buried pain of unfinished family relationships.

What Can We Accomplish Working Together with Spiritual Beings?

In my experience, reinforced by the myriad accounts of psychics and Near-Death Experiences, our loved ones may still have worries, concerns and problems on the other side and we can, with loving communication, help them resolve these lingering struggles. I recall one very powerful dream with my mother in which she cried out in terrible anguished guilt about her role in my emotional struggles. Witnessing her pain, I instantly let go of old grudges knowing how deeply they hurt her and how unprepared she had been to be the kind of mother I needed.

Spirits and humans can also provide love and support for one another, a process easily accessible through dialoguing as illustrated above. Help from ancestors, angels and spirit guides is always available in solving personal problems, healing unfinished business, supporting our mystical activism and influencing real world situations.

Exercise: Reaching Across the Veil

This exercise invites you to have a dialogue with an ancestor, angel or spirit guide of your choosing. Stay open. Begin in your imagination in any way that feels comfortable and meaningful.

As the dialogue unfolds, perhaps the process will change your outlook on communicating with the other side.

1. With paper and pen handy nearby, sit peacefully, quiet your thoughts, and bring your attention inside. Proceed slowly and deliberately through the instructions. No rush, no time limits, no goal other than to experience what happens.

2. Move into mystical consciousness with the keys: stop thinking, heighten sensory awareness and awe, experience the world exactly as it is, and come into Presence to support and safeguard the experience.

3. Reflect on whom you would like to meet and converse with. You may choose a departed loved one, angel or spirit guide. Who do you choose?

4. Write about the individual you're interested in meeting. If a relative, describe your relationship and feelings about this person; if an angel or spirit guide, picture them in your imagination. Be spontaneous, creative, and imaginative. Don't worry about being realistic or objective. Describe the individual's clothes, posture, and expression as vividly as you can. Don't censure, judge or analyze the image in any way.

5. Describe how the presence of this other figure makes you feel. Take your time. Be thorough and complete. What emotions stir inside?

6. Now begin a conversation. Greet the other. Call them by name or ask their name if you don't know it already. How does the figure respond?

7. Explain why you wanted to meet. Ask questions. Write the other's spontaneous responses. Don't analyze, just let the conversation take off and continue for as long as it feels meaningful and unscripted. Be sure you are recording the whole encounter for later reference.

8. When the conversation feels complete or has given you all you can handle, feel free to ask to end the encounter. Say what it meant to you and find a way to say goodbye for the time being.

9. Continue to sit quietly. Review your notes. When you're ready, reflect on this encounter and what you learned.

10. Finally, when you feel complete, stop writing and return to your conventional consciousness and the rest of your day.

I believe that ancestors, spirit guides and angels see and move through our world. In mystical consciousness, we see them with the gift of awakened imagination and can learn to work together to heal each other, gain deeper understanding of our struggles, and change the World of Man. The possibilities are incredible, especially as we discover the wonderful gifts we already have to share.

Chapter 13

What Can I Give? Discerning Our Sacred Gifts for the World

Let's get back to practical considerations for a moment. People frequently experience a desire to "give back" to others, and the world, but are unsure what they have to offer. While the question, "What Can I Give?" appears simple on the surface, superficial answers often do not lead to meaningful engagement, resulting instead in discouragement, disinterest or loss of motivation over time. A thoughtful exploration of our own temperament, values, spirituality and mystical awareness, however, can initiate the deeply meaningful process of *discernment*, exploring ultimate themes of meaning, purpose, and the unrecognized gifts of the true self. This chapter presents a discernment model for uncovering our sacred nature and purpose in the divine world.

Discovering A Calling

We are often exhorted to contribute our time, energy, wisdom and experience in "giving back" to the world in countless ways. We can volunteer at food banks, mentor youth, meditate for world peace, or start discussion groups. We can also pursue political action on causes like climate change, income equality, homelessness, racism, ageism, sexism, sustainable living, education, and world peace. There is virtually no limit to our volunteer opportunities or the world's needs – it's a veritable banquet of choices!

But when I retired, I was surprised by how much resistance I felt to getting involved in these ways. First of all, it felt like going back to work and I was done with the work grind. I didn't want a schedule or obligations. Second, the world's problems seemed so great, the obstacles so big, the answers so elusive, the possibilities so many, I just threw up my hands. Where do I start? What do I do? And finally, there was the problem of finding something that really spoke to me which was more difficult than I imagined, but which may be the most important element of all. I have heard this same struggle from many of my friends and the elders I've met at conscious aging conferences, so I think there is something really important about this search.

The question of how to "give back" did not resolve for me until I finally accepted who I really was and what I really wanted to do. Why is this personal search so important and how do we do it? As theologian Howard Thurman elegantly advised, "Don't ask yourself what the world needs. Ask yourself what makes you come alive, and go do that, because what the world needs is people who have come alive." My goal for the rest of this chapter is to help you answer Howard Thurman's question for yourself. What makes you come alive?

Three Questions

Let's jumpstart our discernment process with three questions.

1. Have you ever had difficulty identifying a meaningful way of "giving back"? How did you deal with this?
2. How often do you "give back" now in some way? Does it seem like enough? Do you feel you are making a difference in the world?
3. Have you ever experienced moments of doubt or burnout in your "giving back" activities where you lost the fire inside? How did it affect you?

If you've wrestled with any of these questions keep reading. If you haven't, read on anyway because you might discover new ways to awaken even more energy, passion and aliveness for what you're doing.

Discernment

As a psychologist, minister, and mystic, I view discernment from a spiritual and depth-oriented perspective implying a prolonged and heartfelt search for one's truest calling and vocation. Why am I here? What did I come here to do? These kinds of questions begin to inspire a heartfelt journey into service.

For most of us, a calling isn't going to involve some huge, lofty or grand enterprise, like ending cancer, war or world hunger. It's different than that. Listen to how Parker Palmer puts it, "Vocation... is something I can't not do, for reasons I'm unable to explain to anyone else and don't fully understand myself but that are nonetheless compelling." It's what you feel compelled by your very nature to do so that you can't not do it. Theologian Frederick Buechner adds this critically important ingredient, stating that vocation is, "the place where your deep gladness meets the world's deep need." What is your deep gladness? And Andrew Harvey wisely counsels to "follow your heart break," suggesting that whatever breaks open your heart is where you are called to serve. Discernment is how we find out what these conundrums mean to us personally.

This sort of sacred self-engagement is also a particularly good focus for conscious elders searching for meaning and purpose in the later years. Indeed, the New Aging – this new developmental stage in the human life cycle – is perfectly suited to finding and expressing this work of the soul. From a spiritual perspective, I believe it's one of the reasons we're living so long in the first place. But the challenge for all of us, young and old, is this: Don't just do what you're told, find out who you really are and what makes you come alive. Because when we don't know who we really are or what unique and precious gifts we bring into the world, it is too easy to join good-sounding causes only later to grow frustrated or burned out. So, the key questions really are, "Do you come alive in your work?" "Is it something you can't not do?" "Does it bring out your deep gladness?" And, "Does it touch a place in your heart that's been opened by another's pain?"

We are each puzzle pieces looking for where we fit in the huge puzzle that is humanity's struggle to heal its wounds and save the planet. Our individual piece is precious and unique, and we need to find out where our piece fits. In fact, when we discover and express our own piece, the puzzle adjusts to our work. Then, wherever we express our gifts will be our place.

Six Factors of Discernment

In exploring any path of service or social, sacred or mystical activism, I believe we need to explore six important discernment factors – factors that will either intensify or diminish our passion and aliveness. If we ignore these factors, we may act in ways that appear helpful but instead cause more problems, betray our true work in the world, and lead to emotional exhaustion. I love what David Nicol, writing on subtle activism, said,

> *I participated in numerous rallies for peace and environmental issues and helped out with a progressive political campaign. Yet amid these efforts, I sometimes wondered how much our activism was truly effective in bringing about the world we desired. Many of the legal and political actions I was involved in, although well intended, seemed only to add to the cycle of reactivity and suffering we were attempting to resolve.*

Nicol's words rephrase the problem cited earlier – when we confront the World of Man from inside the World of Man, that is, when we marshal more arguments and logic, we often contribute to the cycle of conflict. Discernment can lead to a different approach.

Keep in mind that these factors are neither absolute nor mutually exclusive; rather they represent differing points of reference. Also, some factors may have more personal significance to you than others, so pay attention to the moment when a comment or idea sends a jolt of recognition through you, like, "Wow that's me!" and make a note for yourself.

1. The True Self. I know this term is bandied around a lot these days, and sometimes trivialized or ridiculed, but it's really important. As we saw in Heaven's Compass, the true self is who we really are inside, our inborn "given" nature awakened by soul and Presence, that ultimately gives shape to our work in Heaven on Earth. It's hardwired, we don't get a choice on who we were born to be! We may be a high-energy action-oriented person, a quiet, reflective one, a hard-headed or soft-hearted person, a fixer or healer, an artist or intellectual, a mystic or a skeptic, a gardener or academic. We already know a lot about who we really are by how we act naturally and what we love to do. But an old saying adds deeper significance to this realization. It goes, "Who you are is God's gift to you, what you do with it is your gift to God." So, it's not about what we should do, it's about who we really are and what we've been given to do by our very nature.

Whether we use the diagnostic instruments like Myers-Briggs Type Indicator or the Enneagram, seek feedback from our therapist, spiritual director, family or friends, or even just notice when and where we feel happiest, we need to get in touch with our true self. Always protect and cultivate it. Coming home to our essential nature is a profoundly centering act, one that can become an invaluable compass for the rest of our life. And we should never compare our self with anyone else. As the great spiritual teacher Krishnamurti emphasized, personal comparisons are always a form of violence. Instead, in the experience of our true self, we will discover the passion and interests that will lead to the right place to share our gifts.

There are two more facets to the true self we need to honor. The first is this: Tragedies often reveal who we really are, stripping away our social masks and compromises. It's one of the fundamental truths of psychological development. Writing in her 80s, Jungian analyst Florida Scott-Maxwell said,

> *I often want to say to people, "You have neat, tight expectations of what life ought to give you, but you won't get it." That isn't what life does. Life does not accommodate you, it shatters you. It is meant to, and it couldn't do it better. Every seed destroys its container or else there would be no fruition.*

We grow by shattering old forms, the plant breaks its pot, and the true self is revealed in our crises.

And that leads to the second facet of the true self that we must honor: the wounded self. When life cuts us, when we are broken by people, events or circumstances, whether by violence, loss, illness, addiction or crushing defeat, we are asked by the psyche – and the divine – to become wounded healers. Why? Because our wound gifts us with incredible insight, compassion, desire, and energy to help others heal similar wounds. If we are an alcoholic, a rape survivor, an abandoned child, or a victim of gun violence, we may be the perfect choice for giving back the wisdom of our wound – assuming – and this is a huge caveat – that we've worked on it psychologically. The wounded healer archetype takes form only as we work through our own brokenness.

One final suggestion. Bob Atchley, a well-known gerontologist and friend, gave a very useful and practical tip on finding your own work. He said imagine yourself as a tuning fork. If you're in the right place for your soul, that fork will hum. If it's not humming, it's not the right place for you. As you explore the many possibilities of service and activism, see where your tuning fork hums.

2. The Ego-Soul Relationship. As described earlier, soul refers to the spiritual force that gives rise to the true self. True self and soul are two sides of a single coin – one from the psychological realm and the other from the spiritual realm. Remember the Bob Dylan song, *Don't Think Twice, It's Alright*. The person in the song is breaking up with his girlfriend. He explains that he gave her his heart but what she really wanted was his soul, so he left. It's one thing to give your heart, but don't ever give up your soul! And yet we do that all the time, at work, in relationships, and sometimes even in volunteer activities. Decades as a psychotherapist taught me that much of real psychotherapy involves the search and recovery of the lost or abandoned soul expressed as the true self. Why? So we can live our own life and not somebody else's.

As you will recall, ego is the "me" that's in charge. I am writing with the ego's analytic skills. In the long run, the ego's most important job in discernment is to understand and support the soul so that we can share our inborn gifts with the world. That's what Quadrant 2 is all about. When the soul is taken over by someone else's ego and its agenda, or when the ego becomes too attached to our own importance or beliefs and becomes inflated, we lose touch with the soul's vision and purpose, and find ourselves way over in Quadrant 3. Then, we can run busily in endless activities and not achieve anything truly life changing.

Here's the bottom line: An ego disconnected from soul either wants to be told what to do or run the whole show; and the soul apart from ego just wants to love the world and share its gifts but lacks the tools. In reality, they need to work together. This is what Buddhists imply by the phrase "skillful means": It's the ego knowing how to take conscious, intentional, and soulful action to serve the world.

Here's one more really important point. Recall from Heaven's Compass that when we choose the ego over soul in our lives, work or relationships, a self-inflicted emotional wound occurs.

Feeling rejected and unwanted, the true self reacts with anger, sadness, depression or resignation, producing a shadow realm of angry feelings affecting our motivation. Jesus put it this way: "If you bring forth what is within you, what you bring forth will save you. If you do not bring forth what is within you, what you do not bring forth will destroy you." In other words, if we bring forth what is within us – the true self – what we bring forth will save us, helping create a rich and vibrant life of love and service. If we do not bring forth what is within us, what we do not bring forth will undermine what we, as ego, try to accomplish. In fact, when ego moves too far from true self and soul, some form of psychological breakdown or hubris-related catastrophe usually follows, forcing us to acknowledge the terrible mistake we made. Ironically, our emotional symptoms and great failures are the way home. This, too, is discernment.

3. The Introversion/Extroversion Continuum. This continuum represents a pretty obvious but no less important dimension. Some people thrive as extroverts, acting forcefully in the world in leadership roles, social organizing, campaigns, protests, and rallies; they get energy from social connection that feeds them; while others flourish as introverts, working best from their inner life in more solitary roles, one-to-one relationships, small groups, or contemplative forms of activism, such as prayer and visualization; they get energy and inspiration from solitude and deep self-connection.

Of course, no one is purely extrovert or introvert, it's a continuum, but strong preferences need to be recognized. We need to know whether we are an "out there" or "inside" person, for the spheres and means of our "giving back" will vary accordingly. And more importantly, we will be unhappy and ineffective if we're in the wrong place for too long. You can waste a lot of energy being in the wrong place.

Ultimately introverts and extroverts can and should

complement each other. Introverts can help extroverts temporarily postpone action to integrate images and intuitions from the deep Self. The result of this inner focus is a more intuitively centered and mature course of action, not to mention the wisdom of visionary insights. Similarly, extroverts can help introverts express their deep images or intuitions effectively in the world without getting lost in wild ideas or navel gazing. This mutually supportive relationship combats the impulsivity of extroverts and the passivity of introverts, and respects their proper spheres of influence.

At the practical level, this factor also addresses the social structure we are drawn to. Do we prefer to work in large organizations, small work groups, one-to-one relationships, or alone? A healthy organization will make space for all types.

4. The Changing Experience of Age. Across the entire lifespan, aging changes us, changes our life. It's a profound experience. We don't really get to choose whether we age or what things might happen along the way. So, let's look more closely at how this factor affects our giving back.

In general, the young and middle-aged need to be active and goal-oriented. They're busy in the doing mode. They grow through experience and risk-taking, and seek the Hero's Journey beautifully described by Joseph Campbell. This orientation is obvious in the busy lives of our kids, but it also reflects the new inspiration and energies of younger generations. Live from your generation! Each has so much to offer.

Conscious elders, on other hand, who spent a lifetime on this journey of awakening, are full to the brim with wisdom, experience, heart and soul and, as a result, have more access to the being mode. In the being mode, we increasingly act from the richness and depth of our own deeply seasoned nature, trusting the mulch of experience, no longer relying on externally defined goals, strategies, priorities and authorities. This is not our first rodeo! We've been around the block many times. We're like growth rings in a tree.

This doing-being shift grows ever more important with the passage of time. The later years can be roughly divided into three periods: *the young old, the middle old* and *the old, old*. The young old (60-70 or so) don't feel much different than middle-aged folks and often stay more active and goal-oriented. That works for them. The middle old (70 to 80), however, begin to experience limitations of energy, health and physical function that limit their doing activities. For example, now in my seventies, I've had a hip replacement, a shoulder repair, a knee tendon that snaps if I don't do enough exercise, and I live in permanent atrial fibrillation that can be tiring. Facing these kinds of limitations, we are naturally and increasingly drawn to the being mode, like spending quality time with other people and the Earth, opening the heart and being lovingly present to other sentient beings.

Finally, the old, old, defined less by age and more by our degree of frailty and decline, live far more in the being mode. When elders have worked on Secret II, the Transformation of Self and Consciousness, and the depth of love they share is like the light from a Chinese lantern – warm, loving, patient, kind, wise – it goes everywhere and touches everyone Remember the wise book, *Tuesdays with Morrie*? In his profoundly disabled condition, Morrie could do almost nothing but his way of being touched everyone. As we move in our aging from doing to being, we can serve right where we are, and simply by being who we are, and never underestimate how important this is! One of my good friends describes time with his two-year-old granddaughter and how they snuggle in the sun after she's played in the wading pool. He wraps the towel around her and they sit silently in the afternoon sunshine. He says that he has never felt so happy and complete in his whole life.

Of course, there is one major caveat: We don't get wise and loving just by getting old. To gain this kind of depth, we have to do the spiritual work of aging described in Chapter 8. Work on yourself! You'll have so much more to give back if you do.

5. The Status of Archetypal Gender Energies. How we express our gifts can also differ depending on how we use our inborn masculine and feminine energies or potentials, in other words, the archetypal masculine and feminine modes of being we all share.

We have each been given fixed allotments of masculine and feminine energies but we often express them in different ways or orders. People express archetypal masculine energies in competition, quest and conquest. They venture out into the world of ambitions to make their fortune, provide for their families, or take on great causes. People express archetypal feminine energies in nurturing, caretaking and nesting, devoting themselves to nourishing children, family, hearth and home. Of course, we all have and do both but not always as deeply as we wish because of compromises we had to make along the way, particularly balancing work and family.

As we move through life, we begin to search for the unexpressed side of our self. Some of us, having depleted our masculine aggressive energies, now need to express our feminine energies through caretaking and deep being, and others, having spent their feminine side, now need to express more aggressive and action-oriented doing energies. But here's the underlying point. It's always about finding balance and completing the self. If we've ignored or betrayed one side or the other, we may feel the need to develop that side more. Moreover, at this time in history, we are reexamining gender formation and identity, and the value of this exploration is the permission it gives people to find their gender nature earlier, and not waste time conforming to World of Man prescriptions. Archetypes may not change but we are free to live them as we are called.

6. Spiritual Practice. As we have seen, spiritual beliefs and mystical consciousness can have a profound effect in our "giving back" activities, protecting and sustaining us in times of hardship, awakening deeper vision and commitment, and transforming our experience of self and world. Spirituality sets the stage for our engagement. Then, in mystical activism, we immerse ourselves in awakened consciousness, becoming divine humans in a divine world. This perceptual awakening reveals, protects and celebrates Heaven on Earth as our true home and welcomes the energies and visions of soul, prophet, ancestors, angels and spirit guides in the Great Work of Creation. The message here is this: work the spiritual exercises that transform you; change yourself and you will change the world.

I believe that assessing these six factors can help us find our most natural and meaningful way of "giving back." To review, we need to ask ourselves questions like,

- "What are the natural gifts of my True Self?"
- "How well do I, as ego, support my soul in the expression of these gifts?"
- "Am I acting in alignment with my natural introversion or extroversion?"
- "Have I appreciated how age has changed me and welcomed its gifts?"
- "What role have archetypal gender energies played in this new time?"
- "Do my spiritual beliefs and mystical experiences awaken and energize my 'giving back'?"

To further help you find your own best way of giving back, a Discernment Questionnaire can be found in the Appendix. Fill it out and see what else you discover about yourself.

Experiential Exercise

This short experiential exercise invites help from the "other side" for your self-discovery process. Go slowly. Remind yourself to be open to whatever happens.

1. Put down pen and pencil, close your eyes, and just relax.

2. Take a couple of deep breaths and settle comfortably into your chair, your body, your being. Take your time. Let this be a peaceful, gentle, and loving experience.

3. Let your thoughts slow down and come to rest. Release the questions, distractions and issues of the day and center your attention deep inside, descending into the rich dark inner space of self or spirit.

4. Now picture yourself standing by clear pool of water in a quiet place on a lovely day. You might hear birds chirping or a breeze rustling leaves around you. Just be there fully present.

5. You have come to this sacred pool to seek guidance in finding your own best way of "giving back." To help you succeed in this quest, silently call out for any friends, spirits, allies, ancestors, wisdom figures, angels or other beings whose support you value. Who do you want to support you in this inner search? Ask them to come and help you understand and find this work of your soul. Picture them coming forward and standing around the water with you. Feel them joining you, aligning their highest energies with yours.

6. Open also to the deep energies of the sacred Earth that hold and embrace you, to the stars and the cosmos that

sense your existence, and to the divine being, however you conceive it, and feel its loving Presence surround you.

7. Now think of one question the discernment process has stirred in you. Any question you like. Let that question become clear. Now, in the silence of this deep inner space, standing beside this pool, supported by wise and loving beings, silently ask that question and look deeply into the water. Be still and patient. Wait until some kind of answer rises – an image, metaphor, feeling, figure, place – whatever. Take your time.

8. Reflect on what has been revealed. See how it might help you answer your question. Hold it dear. If nothing has come to you, save the image in your soul and wait for a revelation to come later on when the time is right.

9. Now thank the beings who came to help you. Express your love and gratitude for their assistance as they now depart, and feel their gratitude as well for the work you're doing on yourself and in the world.

10. Find your way back to this room, this moment, and your normal experience of self and body, and when you're ready, open your eyes and get reoriented to where we are.

11. Take a moment to reflect on your revelation. How does it fit with your questionnaire responses?

We all have so much to give the world. Like Coyote, we are given unique and wonderful gifts to share, gifts that can be found in the natural ways of our true self incorporating our soul's purpose for incarnating. Who you are most deeply is the gift of self and soul that only you can bring forth. Be yourself and you will be contributing exactly what you came here to do. But the path is never a straight line. To find and express your own way of giving back, you may have to *give up* something you've assimilated from the historical patriarchy.

Chapter 14

The Aging Patriarchy: Coming Home from War

The World of Man is a fundamentally patriarchal structure – that's why I called it the World of Man! Made and maintained by men, it is not inclined toward mysticism. In fact, my first book was initially titled, *Midlife, Masculinity and Mysticism*, but the publisher advised me to rename it because, "Men don't buy books on mysticism." It's probably still mostly true. But the patriarchal enterprise still standing in the way of a sacred world is gradually disintegrating, one mistake, one disaster, one defeat, one lesson, one endless war, one foolish idea at a time as it stumbles home to love. To fully address the mystical dimensions of activism in this apocalyptic time, we need to examine the forces we are up against. The warrior culture will not go down easily.

Coming Home from the Warrior Life

The patriarchy is the collective expression in behavior, attitude and values of ingrained warrior masculinity – men acting synergistically, modeling and reinforcing patterns of nonnegotiable strength, self-sufficiency, reactive aggression, and submission to the alpha male hierarchy. The men's movement of the 90s and recent research reported by the American Psychological Association have documented the psychological harm of these patriarchal values, conferring gender-based privileges to men but also trapping them in narrow, emotion-constricting roles as well as harming women, indigenous peoples, animals and the Earth herself. Many call this scripting "toxic masculinity." While the healthy archetypal masculine envisions strength based on maturity, morality, service, and the hero's journey of psychological and spiritual growth, generations of men have instead been enculturated into dark and exaggerated patriarchal values such as unrelenting conquest, ruthless competition, power and superiority, wealth and exploitation, racism and sexism, war and top-down control.

Global warming, the fast approaching apocalypse roiling waves of chaos and disruption, will shatter the patriarchy's self-serving snow globe, demanding that we transform our ancient instinct for war into a visionary call for peace, survival, science, social justice, spiritual awakening and the mystical renewal of civilization. Interestingly, just such a patriarchy-transforming vision was born in the collective psyche over two millennia ago, hidden in one of the most powerful myths of all.

The Odyssey, transcribed 2,700 ago years by the blind poet Homer, describes humankind's awakening from the corrupt, violent, testosterone-driven, prideful warrior battleground depicted in *The Iliad* to the mature wisdom of age. It is a story of the patriarchy's long slow struggle to achieve a mature awareness of itself, the world, and divinity, and transition from a war-based value system to the enlightened consciousness of the immanent divine as the world itself. This timeless myth, depicting our transformation from raging, blood-thirsty warriors to spiritually and mystically mature wisdom figures, is an ancient gift from the collective unconscious outlining our journey home to love. It is a story of individual and cultural transformation, as pertinent today as it was in ancient Greece, and a revelation of humanity's path to the new world.

The Odyssey describes the developmental tasks men of the patriarchy must confront as they seek to come home to love and Creation. Studying this great tale, I identified 18 developmental tasks of aging and divided them into four categories: *Early Mistakes, Transformational Experiences, Homecoming*, and *Final Challenges*. I'd like to discuss them with you as a way of dreaming the end of a very destructive cultural form.

Because of space constraints, we will briefly touch on only

nine of these adventures but the entire story can be found in the resource material. For male readers, I invite you to visualize each adventure, bring it to life inside, and make notes about how the story might symbolize your journey home. Because it is a recipe for male enlightenment, these lessons from *The Odyssey* will apply to all men. For female readers, try to understand the deeply painful path men and their patriarchy must now take to heal from toxic masculinity. This is not an excuse to forgive the patriarchy; it is an invitation to understand how deeply estranged from self and soul are the men you will encounter in this tale and in your own life.

Background and Adventures

The Odyssey begins after the brutal ten-year Trojan War has finally ended. Odysseus now begins his 500-mile trek from Troy to his family home in Ithaca. He has lost himself in patriarchal grandiosity for a decade, suppressing the heart bonds that matter most. He has not seen his wife in ten years, suitors have taken over his castle, he has never met his son, his mother died in grief, and most fear he has perished. Driven with homesickness, Odysseus begins a journey that shouldn't take more than a few weeks by land or sea, but instead takes him another ten long years, for each adventure symbolizes a different maturational task. These tasks will consume his life, blowing him all over the ancient Mediterranean Sea. The patriarchy's journey home to a mature and loving worldview will be equally demanding and humbling, for retiring the warrior value system runs counter to thousands of years of conditioning.

Early Mistakes

1. Repeating the Past: The Raid on the Cicones. The cruel Trojan War has finally ended. Odysseus and his crew depart for home. The wind takes them first to the south coast of Greece, to a land populated by the Cicones. Odysseus raids a seaport, slaying most of the men, taking women as slaves, and acquiring considerable plunder. Rather than leaving quickly, Odysseus' crew hangs around drinking and slaughtering animals, giving the Ciconians time to send for help. A fierce fighting force soon arrives greatly outnumbering Odysseus' men. In the ensuing battle, Odysseus loses six men and the rest run frantically back to their ships, barely escaping alive.

What's happened here? Nothing has changed. Odysseus is coming home from the war but the first thing he does is start fighting again! He simply continues his warrior ways. How do modern men do that? We golf as if it were a test of personal worth, attempt to be the CEOs of our own homes, start a major remodel of the house for something to direct, or pursue heroic challenges like climbing mountains. We have to succeed, produce, and conquer everything we try. Nothing changes – whatever we do it's more warrior behavior. In this first adventure, the warrior defense is still in place – we haven't even started to grow yet. Does this remind you of anything?

The patriarchy's homecoming follows this same pattern. When one war ends, we look for another. Men plan space travel, arctic domination and powerful new weapons. Knowing that war instantly generates more attention than peaceful times, politicians maintain power by stirring patriotic fervor. Giant corporations conquer one sector of the economy and seek others. Greed and conquest create a kind of hunger that is never satisfied. It's never enough. This unreflective patriarchy is also quick to violence in defense of tribal power, resulting in subtle and openly expressed xenophobic rhetoric and behavior. The more eruptive the response, the more unconscious and dangerous are its foot soldiers no matter how patriotic or rationalized their disguise. It is not surprising, therefore, that Odysseus responds with this kind of automatic and immature cruelty at the beginning of his journey, for the patriarchy represents the dark and toxic masculine so easily exploited by powerful leaders for their own purposes. But as men drive the patriarchy, so too must men dismantle it, and sublimate the underlaying energies to peaceful goals. That's the purpose of coming home and it will only happen if men change.

2. Falling Asleep: The Land of the Lotus-Eaters. Grieving for their lost companions, Odysseus and his men are caught in a violent and supernatural storm. Their ships finally reach land where they rest for two days. Resuming the journey, powerful wind and sea currents drive the ships for ten days, finally depositing them on an island of Lotus-Eaters. The inhabitants of this island share the honey-sweet fruit of the lotus with their visitors. It's basically opium. All who eat this fruit, however, lose the will to work and completely forget about their voyage home. To escape, Odysseus binds his intoxicated men to the masts of the departing ships until they sober up far from the shore.

How do modern men do this? After pursuing various warrior heroics, we kind of fall asleep. Think alcohol, drugs, TV, computer games, surfing the net, compulsive exercise – all sorts of soul-deadening habits. We go unconscious. We get completely sidetracked and forget the purpose of our journey! Does this remind you of anything?

The patriarchy, too, puts men to sleep with dreams of male superiority. It hides the fact that it is only a mind form imposed on young boys early in life: what men are supposed to be. Indigenous cultures created initiation rituals for bringing boys to authentic manhood, rituals intended to reveal their sacred gifts and place in the community. Without such rituals, the need for initiation goes dark, boys drink the patriarchal Kool-Aid, their souls fall asleep for years, and they join the false masculine.

3. Extreme Self-Sufficiency: The Errant Winds. Odysseus and his men arrive next at a floating island enclosed by a rampart of bronze. The island's king, Aiolos, has twelve children, evenly divided between sons and daughters. With no other people on the island, he requires his daughters to be consorts for the sons. Nonetheless his family is wealthy, well fed and live in great houses. The king and his wife entertain Odysseus and his crew for a month, asking many questions about their journey. Eventually Odysseus asks for directions home. As a parting gift, Aiolos gives him a tightly-sealed leather bag holding all the errant winds that might blow his ship off course, leaving only the West Wind to carry them home.

Aided by the West Wind, the men travel swiftly for ten days. Odysseus, anxious to reach home as quickly as possible, refuses to sleep and sails his ship all the way by himself. Just as Ithaca comes into sight, he falls asleep. His men grow curious about the bag and suspect it might hold treasures from King Aiolos. While Odysseus sleeps, the men open the bag, releasing powerful winds that sweep them all the way back to Aiolos' island. When Odysseus discovers what has happened, he is nearly suicidal with grief and remorse. Odysseus returns to Aiolos' castle and begs for the king's assistance once again. This time, instead of embracing Odysseus, the king orders him to leave the island, proclaiming that any man whom the gods punish with such bitterness will not receive his help.

Here we meet a king and his family who appear to be totally self-contained on an island with impenetrable ramparts. Even the children marry each other, needing no other suitors, and everything is provided for them. This land is a powerful symbol of narcissistic self-sufficiency: the idea that a man can – and should! – handle everything by himself. Build gated communities, need no one, increase your wealth. That the island is untethered suggests that this defensive attitude is ungrounded; the inhabitants' strength comes not from a connection to the deep Self but instead from rigid and superficial standards of self-sufficiency.

So it is that Odysseus, from this position of self-sufficiency, insists that he sail the ship single-handedly for ten days without sleep. Fueled by grandiosity and sheer willpower, he is once again the compulsive warrior doing it all. Odysseus falls asleep because he is, in fact, not emotionally ready to be home given all the chaotic and immature emotions he has stuffed in the bag. The men who break into Odysseus' bag represent the greediness behind this grandiosity. What's the moral? Self-sufficiency is not the answer to aging. Does this remind you of anything?

Patriarchies, attached to wealth, power and superiority, rationalize that self-sufficiency is the key to success. Pick yourself up by the bootstraps. Overcome every obstacle. Be ruthless and unforgiving. Take control. In its extreme form, this attitude has no room for genuine compassion, intimacy, friendships, community, or cultural diversity. To paraphrase Paul Simon, we are a rock, we are an island, and an island feels no pain – for anyone.

Transformational Experiences

4. Coming to Terms with the Feminine: Circe the Witch. Odysseus and his crew come to this island where a beautiful witch turns men into pigs with a magic potion. There's a metaphor! How do men act like pigs around beautiful women? Think flirtation! Think sex! Think hormones! Think male competition! With the help of Hermes, however, Odysseus takes a medicine that prevents her magic drink from working. He fearlessly consumes her drug, confronts her power, goes to bed with her as equals, and then insists she turn his men back into human beings. A great feast follows.

What does this adventure symbolize? This is where Odysseus begins to confront his long-established male attitude toward women. Now instead of objectifying and sexualizing them, which would turn him into a pig, he consciously prevents his own sexual intoxication, addresses his underlying fear of women without acting out, and finally insists on an honest relationship with Circe. No more games! This is important stuff for men! How do we need to see women as true equals and guides? Interestingly, the feminine presence is constantly helping Odysseus: Athena, Circe, Calypso, Penelope, and many others, and it's not about sex. Can you relate to this?

The theme of power-based sexual objectification and manipulation, of course, is central to the patriarchy and maintains its hold in gender inequality. Whether it's pay, power, or porn, government, corporations and religions have always been male dominated and the costs have been detrimental to women, families and the culture in so many ways. Gender equality, on the other hand, reflects the absolute unity of all beings in Creation.

5. Facing Death: Descent into Hades. Circe wisely advises Odysseus that he needs to visit Hades next. This is the Greek version of hell. There he meets various fallen heroes, many of whom are now painfully regretful of their behavior, his deceased mother who died of a broken heart over his absence and reveals how his wife and son have suffered in his absence, and a blind seer who gives him a prophecy about his last task. Near the end of his visit, however, the spirits of the dead become so terrifying and frenzied that Odysseus and his men run desperately from the mouth of Hades.

What is this adventure about? This is Odysseus' descent into the personal and collective unconscious where he must confront his past, his regrets, the costs of his values and the culture's values, and the reality of death. This is his descent into the Darkness described in Heaven's Compass where old violations, betrayals and wounds are buried. We must all examine our personal past, all we've hidden in the unconscious and what our life has really meant. This is the work of emotional maturation –

looking back, understanding what happened, asking forgiveness and making amends. We can't go forward until we've faced the life we've already lived, for as we have seen, old wounds inevitably imprison us in the World of Man. Though he runs away feeling overwhelmed, Odysseus has actually faced a lot. What do you need to face in your journey home?

The patriarchy must also face its historical sins and its role in bringing on the climate disaster through greed, corruption, and unbridled power. Global warming will be an unforgiving sentence and a moral accounting of the patriarchy's rule. Many were placed in hell through its commitment to inequality and injustice; it's time now for the patriarchy to own its excesses and seek redemption in turning from toxic to enlightened masculinity.

Homecoming Challenges

6. Saying Goodbye to the Goddess: Leaving Calypso. After his ships are destroyed by Zeus for violating the rules of a sacred island, Odysseus is rescued by a beautiful goddess who falls in love with him and offers him eternal life with her if he will be her husband. Although the relationship works for a while – 7 years actually! – Odysseus begins to pine terribly for his wife and begs to leave. Calypso eventually understands his pain and helps him build another raft to sail onward.

What does this adventure mean? Calypso is the divine feminine. Her love has been profoundly healing for Odysseus, which is why he stayed so long. But it can't be the end. Love heals so we can deepen our relationships with real people. If we stay too long in idealized settings, love will become fraudulent. Calypso may be the "perfect woman" and her island the "perfect place," but she is not his real wife and this island is not his real home or life. We can find all sorts of "perfect" scenarios (gated communities, expensive cars, fancy restaurants, ocean voyages, exciting affairs) but they are not home. Odysseus chooses his real wife, family and home over all these distractions. He is gradually maturing. Does this connect for you?

The patriarchy, too, hangs onto false love and security through wealth, power, and corruption, but this, too, is empty love for there is no heart or emotional union in it. As the world collapses in this upcoming climate apocalypse, the patriarchy will break down and men will long for their own salvation in real community. Wealth hoarders, power hierarchies and narcissism, all must go; only lovers, healers and helpers can create the new community. We can see feminine values coming to the fore now, values of inclusion, caring, sharing, and working together as one family. Gender injustice must be righted for our survival.

7. Cleansing the Psyche: Confronting the Suitors. Odysseus finally gets back to Ithaca and finds his palace overrun by countless suitors who want to win Penelope's hand in marriage to take over his kingdom, for everyone but Penelope assumed that Odysseus was dead. Each suitor symbolizes an area where Odysseus' warrior impulses still hold his soul captive. As his soul mate, Penelope represents his soul and she is not at all free to be herself, nor is he. With the help of his son, Telemachus, and several loyal servants, Odysseus slays all the suitors. It's a huge and bloody battle.

Aging men need to do likewise, pulling up the weeds of their residual warrior habits. We need to uproot all those invidious, competitive, and narcissistic impulses that still thrive in our psyche and try to take over home and hearth. Instead, we need only to let love in and reconcile with the real and the archetypal feminine we betrayed in our heroic quests. Have you noticed such residual warrior impulses in yourself, desires to conquer and control the home instead of share it?

Like the suitors, vestiges of the patriarchy system will also fight back to hold onto control, believing that a rigged system and the threat of violence can still work. The temptation to restore the old order of white men in power will be great, and battles will be fought, but in the end, it will fail. A new multicultural masculinity, one wedded to the feminine as partner and mate, will inform humanity's coming community. The new world will be homesteaded by love.

Final Challenges

8. Accepting the Reality of Old Age: Visit with Laertes. Odysseus then goes to visit his aged father, and finds him working in an orchard on the estate. At first his father looks like a servant: he's dirty, wears laborer's clothes, toils in the orchards. But then Odysseus notices that his father is actually quite happy and content in this work.

What's happening here? Symbolically Odysseus' father is harvesting the fruits of his lifetime and caring for the Earth. He has, in effect, returned to the Garden, one of the Three Secrets of Aging, and made peace with the nature of old age. How have you found a new kind of peace and fulfillment tilling the garden of life?

Can the patriarchy also grow old, make peace with itself, and dissolve itself into a new consciousness of Earth, community and love? Can it erase its self-importance and just be guys growing old? The patriarchy, like a dinosaur, grew too big, dangerous and foolish. As men wake up, they will be grateful to replace their former careers with jeans, soul mates, family, and community. As the Earth is our only lifeboat. We will revere her again.

9. Finding Holy Ground: Ritual for the Gods. The blind seer in Hades previously told Odysseus that he had one more journey to make when he was home. He was to travel inland until he finds someone who mistakes his oar for a winnowing fan. On that spot, he has to sacrifice a ram, a bull and a boar to Poseidon

– whose son the Cyclops he blinded earlier in the story – and then make individual offerings of cattle to every god in the Greek pantheon.

What is this adventure about? First of all, it's a journey *inland* – to an inner realm. The oar is a symbol of masculine power, which he is to transform. The winnowing fan, used to separate wheat from chaff, symbolizes the process of discernment – the ability to separate what is important from what is not, what is dead and what is alive, the husks of warrior masculinity from the seeds of soul and new growth. The three animals represent the masculine instincts of sex and aggression, which he must sacrifice. And the offerings to the gods symbolize his recognition that he must honor all facets of divinity for his own spiritual maturation. The specific symbols, of course, come from Odysseus' culture but they are, nonetheless, timeless and universal in their ultimate significance. This ritual marks the initiation of his spiritual journey, his transformation of self and consciousness, and his gradual awareness of the divine in the world. Have you turned inward to discern the seeds of your own new spiritual growth in this new and final chapter of your life? What have you found?

As the patriarchal establishment disappears, the crystallized beliefs structuring the World of Man will go, too, for they were always one and the same. Thought will then assume its rightful place as part of the divine mind, and we will increasingly draw from its creativity and intelligence to build a new civilization. As mystical consciousness grows, answers to questions will come spontaneously from the divine mind and all will have access to God's mind in creating this new life. All this will happen without planning or calculation, for it is the natural state of mystical consciousness through the seasons and cycles of life.

These are nine of the eighteen challenges men and the pervasive patriarchy must address on the long journey home to love, wisdom and mystical awakening. The first five ask a man to face his central problem – himself and his patriarchal system. The next five offer a remedy for these problems – a set of transformational experiences that progressively dissolve his egocentric male reactivity and culture into a more mature masculinity. Five more bring the traveler home at last, his psychological, cultural and spiritual transformation finally paving the way for authentic human love. And in the final three challenges, a man makes peace with old age, the world, and divinity, opening a new and peaceful stage of life on Earth. In sum, our collective masculinity must be dismantled and transformed if we are to survive to see the world through mystical eyes. As *The Odyssey* depicts, this journey will not be easy, much will be lost, but humanity may again discover that the beauty and divinity of Creation are still here, if we can come home from war and ready ourselves for humanity's greatest challenge – the coming chaos of the Dark Night of Civilization.

Chapter 15

Chaos, Descent, Awakening, Rebirth: Welcoming a New World

Most religions prophesize the coming of a savior and the spiritual awakening of humanity. What they did not fully realize in their original prophecies is that the world savior is you and me and that we are all called to be Divine Humans in a Divine World. Mystical consciousness opens the door to this final realization and mystical activism lights the way forward.

This book is about changing the world in a most unusual way – by transforming ourselves. When we awaken the power of mystical consciousness, we walk into a radiant and breathtakingly precious new world right before our eyes. Once again recalling the words of Joseph Campbell, "The end of the world is not an event to come, it is an event of psychological transformation, of visionary transformation. You see not the world of solid things but a world of radiance."

In awakened consciousness, our thought-projected problems and issues disappear in a flow of divine perception and open-hearted being. We return to Garden consciousness in deep communion with the all-pervading divine. Mystical activism is not about changing the World of Man, it's about dissolving it in the direct perception of Creation as our truest home and then dwelling in a loving, all-inclusive, and all-conscious blending of Heaven and Earth. We achieve this end through our own mystical self-transformation and by employing the multiple tools of mystical consciousness – awakened perception, Heaven's Compass, dialogues with the other side, and experiential exercises – to revolutionize the way we respond to crisis, hardship and loss. In the process, we awaken a new kind of human being and a new human culture.

I also believe Campbell's visionary transformation reveals that the next stage of our spiritual evolution is already happening right now, right before our eyes, evident in all the transitions described in preceding chapters – from spirituality to mysticism, left-brain thinking to right-brain consciousness, personality to Presence, patriarchy to new aging, false self to divine human, soul to prophet, and, with a little help from our friends on the "other side," from the World of Man to Heaven on Earth. Together we join humanity's great pilgrimage into our evolutionary future. But the road will be rocky.

The Dark Night of Civilization

The 2016 presidential election triggered an unexpected and nearly unbearable trauma for over half of the American people. For many, it felt like the death of a loved one, or the assassinations of John Kennedy, Martin Luther King, and Robert Kennedy, or the nightmare of 9/11. It felt like a wrecking ball shattering our nation's fragile architecture of decent human values, urgent plans for climate action, and steadily expanding civil rights. Then things got worse. Not only did the emerging politics challenge the very essence of our humanity, escalating global warming is now delivering unprecedented crises – severe weather, year-round fire seasons, catastrophic flooding, global famine and desperate immigration. End times. Disbelief, shock, grief, tears, fear, insomnia, and fragmented psyches all across the country and around the world, yet many still cling to a denial of its horrific magnitude. It is the same denial that keeps us from facing our own death.

We don't even see the edge yet. Sadly, as history teaches, humanity does not change through grave warnings and great insights, we change through failure and defeat, that is, when we have no other choice. The mystical experience represents an exception to this rule, but even here, we may change our deep knowing but not our character flaws and still retreat back into the false security of the World of Man. Where does that leave the mystical realization of the divine world? It will only be witnessed on a large scale as our grandiosity fails and the house of cards that is the World of Man falls.

The Dark Night of Civilization represents the breakdown of the patriarchal World of Man and our collective descent into the suffering, loss, disorientation and unknowing of Quadrant 4 – Darkness. It also reflects a macrocycle in Heaven's Compass, the cycle of civilization. History also describes the corrosive effects of corruption, abuse of power, debauchery and the suffering of the poor that lead to breakdown, revolution, and eventually new beginnings. We are in just such a time right now only the stakes are ultimate. It is an apocalypse of our own making, yet in this same disrupted ground grow mystical seeds of hope and renewal. Ironically, our hope lies in the emergency itself.

Mysticism in the Age of Apocalypse

Here is a surprising and hopeful truth: Crises awaken mystical consciousness. Emergency consciousness evokes the same intense, wide-awake, "Oh my God!" here-and-now awareness that returns us to the immediate sensory present. We let go of beliefs, schedules, life goals, identities, retirement portfolios, or political views, and return to the urgency of the present and the timeless, awakened consciousness of divinity. We see versions of this principle, for example, during motor vehicle accidents where time suddenly slows down and consciousness transforms perception, in the complete life review experienced by mountain climbers during fifteen seconds of free fall, in a soldier's unplanned heroism in war where he transcends his preoccupation with the false self to save another, and in all manner of Near-Death Experiences where dying is reconceived as a profound religious process. In all these crisis-related altered states, the insecure little self falls away and we experience the awakening of consciousness and the power of love driving a new kind of response. As Rachel Naomi Remen observes, "The daily fabric that covers what is most real is commonly mistaken for what is most real until something tears a hole in it and reveals the true nature of the world."

The collapse of civilization, of the World of Man, represents an opportunity to return to our original consciousness. When our house burns down or a tsunami destroys our village, we hold onto each other, our family, pets and livestock, and do whatever we can for each other. Because emergency consciousness and mystical consciousness are the same thing – one of the greatest paradoxes on the spiritual journey – crises bring profound opportunities for awakening. In the moment of crisis, we can literally step into God's consciousness and act from a divine flow of love and compassion. We become God in action. The primary enemies, of course, are falling back into the left-brain's black-and-white catastrophic thinking, turning against each other, or losing hope, all of which create Hell on Earth. We walk the razor's edge.

Here are our mystical marching orders: When crisis and hardship prevail, stop thinking, heighten awareness, experience the world exactly as it is, come into Presence, and feel the Being of your being. Then do what comes spontaneously from within this awakened state of sacred oneness – help, save, repair, share, love, pray. Let Presence be medicine for broken hearts and broken spirits. Reconnect with soul, ancestors, spirit guides and angels for assistance in coping with the inevitable hardship, pain and suffering we will have to bear. Respond to "problems" with the mystical revelations of Heaven's Compass. Share your gifts as a divine human in a divine world, trusting the constant unfolding, moment-by-moment, of divine revelation. You are not in charge, you are in the great tide of spirit renewing the world.

Our Destination: A New Human Consciousness
Abraham Maslow, the father of humanistic psychology's "Third

Force" of American psychology and its wonderfully enlivening concepts – "hierarchy of needs," "peak experiences," and "self-actualizing personality" – suffered a severe heart attack in his early 60s and died several months later. In the intervening months, a time of very fragile health he called his "post-mortem life," Maslow's personality changed dramatically, shifting from a nearly workaholic level of ambition and productivity to a steady state of transcendent calm, characterized by a deep serenity, unitive consciousness, spontaneous spiritual insights, and pervasive perceptions of radiance, beauty, and the miraculous nature of being. He described this state as the way the world would look if a mystical experience settled into a persistent state.

This experience changed Maslow. He now viewed humanistic psychology as a transitional state, a preparation for a higher transpersonal or trans-human one, a "Fourth Force" in psychology, one that could be taught and intentionally evoked. He called this new state of consciousness the *"plateau experience"* and said he could now awaken it voluntarily and remain "turned on." He talked of teaching "classes in miraculousness."

Pierre Teilhard de Chardin, the French philosopher, paleontologist, Catholic priest, and mystic, coined the term "noosphere" to describe what he sensed as an emerging collective level of unity consciousness, a superintelligence infusing all of us with trans-human awareness and intelligence. Aldous Huxley, too, suggested that an awakened intelligence was coming that would allow humans to transcend their individuality, accelerating a curve of spiritual evolution. I believe Maslow, Teilhard de Chardin, and Huxley were describing an enduring state of mystical consciousness that will evolve one day for all of us. It will be a continuous mystical experience of Creation, transforming our lives and our work, and erasing the artificial mental boundaries depicted in Heaven's Compass.

I'm proposing that mystical consciousness, our long-forgotten but fundamental human capacity for the direct perception of

Creation, can be one of the most important resources for healing ourselves and the psychic split that is destroying our world. Indeed, the World of Man is opening into Heaven on Earth even as you read this. This approaching apocalypse may be the turning point in human civilization, moving us from sins of greed, power and false self, to the all-infusing love and unity of divine reality. This is not the end; it is a call to grow in sacred consciousness, love, courage, goodness and wisdom. We are in this for the long run.

So I beg you, don't read this book, say it's interesting, put it on the bookshelf, and forget it. Use it. Transform yourself over and over again. Risk. Share it with others. We must each transform the World of Man with mystical consciousness before the World of Man destroys us. This is where our spiritual evolution is heading. Step up in the coming crisis. The vision is here, the tools are here, what's missing is personal transformation – yours and mine. And remember, discouragement simply represents a Quadrant 4 state caused by Quadrant 3 thought. Dissolve it with Heaven's Compass and come home to Creation.

The Powers of Mystical Activism

Mystical activism starts with the individual. Each of us needs to experience the transformed consciousness of the mystic and use its powers to transform the world. Those powers include...

Mystical Consciousness. Revelation is itself mystical activism. In the awakened, thought-free experience of Presence, we experience the awe-inspiring beauty and divinity of each other and the world directly. Our vision is radically changed. Shocked, challenged and ultimately thrilled, we discover the possibilities of a new kind of life. From the first glimpse of Heaven on Earth, we work to transform personal and collective perception. Identity, time and story fade into the increasing light of consciousness and we divinize our work and organizations through sustained mystical experience. All that stands in the way is thought.

Personal Transformation. While we might not immediately recognize our own transformation as a mystical power, our awakened state affects the consciousness of those around us and the world itself. Awakening is contagious, for all consciousness is one, and as we raise our own consciousness, we raise the collective field of consciousness. Just as joy and anger are contagious, so too is awakening, only more so. Moreover, the true self, newly inspired in the divine world, literally lives and acts from a state of divine being, sharing its gifts and revelations with others and profoundly touching all sentient beings with unlimited love. In new and disarming ways, we become what we have been seeking: divinity acting in a divine world. Be that. Trust that.

Powerful New Tools for Mystical Activism. Based on the split structure of the human psyche, Heaven's Compass represents a powerful tool for erasing the illusion of a false self in a false world, seeing through self-generated problems, transforming consciousness, mobilizing our inborn capacity for love and service, and helping others do the same. Dialogues with divinity, ancestors, spirit guides and angels can provide additional encouragement and creativity in addressing social problems and crises. Through the mystical portal in the brain's right hemisphere, we welcome the support, guidance and assistance of loving beings who then, through us, move into our world, dissolving the split between sacred and secular realities, promoting mutual healing, dissolving the ossified patriarchy, and inspiring new relationships. All this is available to us every day. Don't go back to sleep.

Soul. As our awakening proceeds, we come upon a surprising new force of energy and activism – soul! Its power pushes each of us to wake up to the divinity everywhere. Soul embodies our future and highest self, bringing new gifts to the world and a new understanding of our work. Lending our voice to this other self, we act boldly through the mystic-to-prophet transformation. Make friends with your soul.

These powers change us. Perception awakens to the beauty and perfection of a divine world. Its light shines through everything. We discover that we, too, are made of God, filled with ecstasy, wonder and love, and we move naturally as if in a divine tide. We love everyone and everything. We communicate with sacred beings in this world and beyond, including those still imprisoned in horrific beliefs and wounded identities. We see divinity in everyone and our seeing changes them. As divinity's conscious being in action, we are fierce with soul and possess new tools for changing self and world. We now do what we came here to do yet remain in the deep state of peace that underlies the chaos of the illusory world.

This transformation is neither linear nor logical, its effects neither predictable nor controllable, its magic neither explainable nor reducible. And most importantly, we are not in charge – such a relief! We enter the new world and hold the door open for others. Though a single thought can take us temporarily back into the World of Man, mystical consciousness always restores Heaven on Earth. The work continues but the reward is a divine life and a new humanity. In this way, we can all reach for the next stage of our spiritual evolution and lift the veil between the worlds.

One More Example

Here is an example of this awakened shift in consciousness. In 1958, Christian mystic, Thomas Merton, had this vision on a street in downtown Louisville. He recalled,

... at the corner of Fourth and Walnut, in the center of the shopping district, I was suddenly overwhelmed with the realization that I loved all these people, that they were mine and I theirs, that we could not be alien to one another even though we were total strangers. It was like waking from a dream of separateness, of spurious self-isolation in a special world... This sense of liberation from an illusory difference was such a relief and such a joy to me that I almost laughed out loud... as if the sorrows and stupidities of the human condition could overwhelm me, now that I realize what we all are. And if only everybody could realize this! But it cannot be explained. There is no way of telling people that they are all walking around shining like the sun. Then it was as if I suddenly saw the secret beauty of their hearts, the depths of their hearts where neither sin nor desire nor self-knowledge can reach, the core of their reality, the person that each one is in God's eyes. If only they could all see themselves as they really are. If only we could see each other that way all the time. There would be no more war, no more hatred, no more cruelty, no more greed... But this cannot be seen, only believed and "understood" by a peculiar gift.

I believe Merton's "gift" is mystical consciousness and its impact is mystical activism.

One More Exercise

We separate ourselves from Creation all the time. Cell phones, computers, Internet, social media, video games, 24-hour online news, clocks and television hold us prisoners in the World of Man. Imagine a month-long wilderness retreat without these mental distractions. In the immediacy of nature, after our "withdrawal" from technology addiction, we would rediscover Creation. It's everywhere! Returning to our senses, heightening our awareness, looking intensely, we would *experience* the divine world that we've been avoiding. This is why we go into nature in the first place as hikers, campers, river rafters and mountain climbers: we intuitively know the healing transformation of the living divine world. And she will also talk to us.

We dialogue with soul, ancestors, spirit guides, and angels, why not trees, animals, minerals and mountains? If we want to know how to support the healing of Creation, let's go to Creation herself. Activating our dialogue skills, we can ask the insects, rabbits, eagles and forests how they feel, what they need, and how we can help them. We create a spiritual practice of returning to the church of nature, praying for guidance from the divine Mother. Repeatedly washing the World of Man from consciousness, we return with a healthier balance of left and right hemispheres. We infuse thought with sacred consciousness and evolve a new kind of humanity and a new civilization.

Yes, we are busy. But the Garden is everywhere. Look out your window. Where does the green begin? Find the path back to Creation and dwell there on a daily basis. Dialogue with a tree. This, too, is mystical activism. Find your Heaven here.

My Final Message to You

My lifetime of study and the wisdom of age can all be distilled to this:

Stop. Stop talking, stop thinking, stop whatever you are doing. We are standing right now in Heaven on Earth. Reality is conscious and alive. It knows us. Divinity is everywhere and everything. We don't see this because we only see our thoughts that create another world, a world that is crazy and ugly. Stop everything, wake up, and SEE. When the ego goes, thought goes, beliefs go, false self and false world evaporate, and the whole house of cards falls apart to reveal that we never left the Garden. We are divine beings in a divine world – pure consciousness, joy, beauty and love. The Self now rises inside like a great tide, filling us with so much joy that all darkness dissolves. And in the great unity of being, I am you, you are me, we are God. This is the "other world." Live in awakened consciousness and know that we are loved, guided and protected no matter what appears to be happening by World of Man standards. As a mystical activist, step into the new world right where you are. This consciousness will transform everything you do and it is contagious. Now, from the depths of conscious divine being, go do the impossible. The pathless path of transformation is simply the next step.

Blessings,
John

Appendix

Discernment Questionnaire: Finding Your Calling

What follows is a list of questions based on the discernment factors. The questions apply to whatever "giving back" activity you're already engaged in or one you might be considering. There are three questions for each factor. Write your responses in your journal. Most importantly, be as truthful as you can because you'll gain the most real personal knowledge that way. Finally, there are no right or wrong answers, only your answers, so don't censor or judge yourself! Here are the questions. Let yourself be surprised by what you discover.

True Self

1. Describe your true self with five adjectives. Who are you most deeply? Remember you're describing your real self, not the social role or mask you wear.
2. List the gifts contained in these qualities. These gifts may not correspond to your education or experience; they refer to your natural and spontaneous nature.
3. Are your gifts being meaningfully expressed in the "giving back" work you're now doing or thinking of doing? Explain.

Ego-Soul Relationship

1. How do you, as ego, support or betray true self and soul in the "giving back" activity you're doing or thinking of doing? Is your ego too powerful or do you surrender your Soul too easily?
2. In your work or everyday life, how do you need to

express your True Self more?

3. What does your soul want most from you in this time of your life?

Introversion-Extroversion Continuum

1. Are you mostly an introvert or extrovert? Explain.

2. Are you drawn to large organizations, small working groups, one-to-one work, or no organization preferring to work alone? Explain.

3. Is your style a good fit with the "giving back" work you're now doing or thinking of doing?

The Changing Experience of Age

1. Have you begun to notice age-related changes in energy, values, or longings? What are you noticing?

2. How do these changes affect the "giving back" activity you're doing or thinking of doing?

3. Where are you in the transition from doing to being?

Archetypal Gender Energies

1. Overall, have you lived your life more from masculine or feminine energies?

2. Which energies call to you most powerfully in your life and giving back activities?

3. Does the work you're doing or thinking of doing support or discourage these new emerging energies?

Spiritual Beliefs and Mystical Experience

1. Do your religious and spiritual beliefs contribute to the "giving back" activity you're doing or thinking of doing? How?

2. Where does mystical consciousness fit in your "giving back"? Where might you deepen the mystical dimension of your life?

3. Can you imagine the "giving back" activity you're doing or thinking of doing becoming a spiritual or mystical practice itself? How?

Now go back over your answers and see what you've discovered. Write down any insights that seem important. What themes keep recurring in your responses?

What Else Can We Do? Responding to Crises in Five Dimensions

What can we do in traumatic times like these? How can we respond? As a psychologist, interfaith minister, mystic and writer on conscious aging, I see this impending crisis in five dimensions: survival, psychological, spiritual, the wisdom of the Sage, and the mystical. Let's spend some time in each of the remaining dimensions and then see where we end up. As we proceed through this material, read slowly, ponder each idea and suggestion, notice how you respond inside, and let yourself be changed. This chapter is a call for personal growth and awakening.

The Survival Dimension
Obviously we need to survive first – water, food, shelter, medicine, safety. The more we can prepare in advance, the better our chances of survival. Science, technology, and government will also be critical and much is already being put in place as the drama builds. Most importantly, we will need to work together, to share, cooperate, and create functioning and sustainable local systems for basic needs. This first dimension exceeds the scope of this book but all are encouraged to plan now.

The Psychological Dimension
This degree of impending trauma is frankly distressing when we finally lift the lid of denial. Its scale is terrifying and will cut deeply. In traumatic circumstances, we are tempted to explode in rage, run away, or go numb in denial, responses consistent with our deepest animal instincts of fight, flight, or freeze. A fourth emotional response is simply to collapse as hope dwindles. None of these responses will solve our problem. We need to process our distress instead, to work on it until we have a clearer and

more stable sense of what the problem really is and what we need from each other. Here are some ideas on managing the psychological dimension of crisis survival. While some of these ideas will seem obvious, they need to be said out loud in order to be prepared.

- What we need most in the beginning is to support each other with compassion and understanding, to hold our shattered and frightened hearts until some basic healing begins. With each great loss or disorientation, we are, for a time, too broken and traumatized to act constructively.
- We need to feel our feelings. Let yourself experience the full range of emotion. Feelings are not reality but they need to be processed if we are to act effectively. Don't be impatient or critical with yourself or others; we are all struggling, we are doing the best we know how at this moment.
- While reactive behavior toward perceived "enemies" can discharge emotion, it is counterproductive in crisis circumstances, causing recurring cycles of reactivity on all sides. When all the acting out is done, we'll still have to deal with the underlying pain.
- Remember that anything you feel changes as you feel it. That's what "working through" means. More importantly, you'll see the situation more clearly as painful emotions heal and release their energy for constructive planning.
- Working through releases our emotional energy for new tasks.
- Working through also involves seeking new insights into oneself and others. What does our emotional reaction say about our values, assumptions and beliefs, and what else may be going on inside us and in our country that is important but not obvious? New insights catalyze new ways of thinking that can move us beyond reactivity into

greater psychological understanding.

- We need to create and remain in community and not isolate ourselves in fortresses of fear. We need each other more than ever. Divided, we cower, together we can be an amazing force of healing, creativity and commitment.

- Working through trauma at the personal and community levels inevitably takes time – in this case, it will take many years. Stay with it. Our lives and communities grow as we process this struggle together.

- Continually assess reality. What's happening right now? How are things changing? Which issues are fading and which are growing? Reality is evolving too. When the time comes, action needs to be grounded in an objective awareness of actual circumstances.

The Spiritual Dimension

One of the gifts of spirituality, however, is that it can provide a framework of hope and values to support us in times of crisis. Here are some ideas for working in the spiritual dimension:

- Ask yourself big questions like, "What are my ultimate spiritual beliefs about what's happened?" "What is the spiritual significance of all this?" "What might our shared traumatization and polarized relationships suggest about humanity's spiritual evolution?"

- Take some time to wonder what the world's great religious teachers would tell us about this situation and how we should respond to it.

- Return to your spiritual practices, like prayer, meditation, and yoga. Your inner stability will be restored as the mind settles and you ground yourself once again in your spiritual values.

- Let your beliefs and practices awaken the love, compassion and courage inherent in your spirituality. Realize that this struggle now engages your spiritual practice.

- Ask yourself, "What is my spiritual purpose or work here?" Write at least ten responses and then see which ones feel the most valid.

The Sage's Wisdom

We introduced conscious elders in Chapter 8. As our civilization grows older, we acquire the gifts of age. From their accumulated wisdom, conscious elders find the authority of the transpersonal voice, a voice that speaks for humanity, all sentient beings, and the future we create for coming generations. Depending on one's Sagely talents, the conscious elder may be a wisdom keeper, historian, healer, mentor, teacher, mystic, prophet, or protector of ultimate values. Here are some ideas for working in the Sage's dimension:

- Review all you have learned about enlightened aging throughout your life. Use these insights to become your best and most mature self. This is the self that evolves into the Sage, the self that can act maturely in the world.
- Enter the awakened consciousness of the Sage by using the keys: Stop thinking for a moment, heighten sensory awareness, and open your capacity for awe. In this state of radical awe, sense the Presence all around you. As your consciousness expands, trust your own knowing – the wisdom, love, joy and compassion that arise in this mystical experience. Notice how differently the world and its problems appear in this state.
- Find your own voice but speak for all beings. Speak clearly, calmly, consciously. Speak with a moral voice. Stand behind your words.
- Apply the unique gifts and talents that make up your True Self to the challenges we now face. Find out what brings you alive and do that for the world.

- Use the savvy acquired in sixty, seventy, eighty or more years of life to approach problems from a higher perspective. This is not your first rodeo. You've seen this before. Be present more than action-oriented in the beginning, skillful more than confronting, and let your doing come from deep being.

- If you're not an elder, use the life experience you have acquired so far and act from the best and highest self you can muster. Wisdom is not limited only to conscious elders.

- Use non-adversarial communication and deep listening. Don't talk at or over people, listen with your heart and ask deep and sincere questions. Let everyone participate in creating solutions.

- Build loving community with all people, friends, strangers and adversaries alike.

- Grow into a Divine Human filled with love. Stand for love.

The Mystical Dimension

This book, *Mystical Activism*, *is* the fifth dimension. Go deep, drink from the waters of sacred consciousness, use Heaven's Compass, reach across the veil, and let this dimension transform all you do in the world. Trust the divinity of your own nature.

How to Live on Five Levels

I hope you are beginning to see the immense resources available to all of us from these five dimensions of experience. We are neither helpless nor alone. In fact, every thought and action now become sacred, every possibility filled with divine potential for healing and transformation.

Here are some final ideas for working in all five dimensions:

- Use the resources available in each dimension to address your experience of trauma. What are you learning? How are you changing?

- Try not to use one dimension to avoid another (for example, thinking that Presence will fix things without your involvement or that being a sage means you won't hurt anymore); that never works for long. Conversely don't ignore any dimension for each contributes something incredibly valuable for coping with trauma.

- With each new development in this national drama, move again through the five dimensions, returning to the work of survival, psychological awareness, spiritual meaning, Sagely wisdom, and mystical consciousness.

- Distrust simple and reactive answers. We are multifaceted beings in a multidimensional world – simple and impulsive answers are nearly always suspect.

- Work in all dimensions concurrently to evolve a plan for mature action. Eventually they will blend into one. Then you're ready. Then you know who you really are and what you must do.

- Stay in community. Share your feelings. Support others. Love the world and assist the whole human family in solving its problems. We will only succeed if we all succeed.

Source Material: A Brief Summary of My Work

I have been following a singular mystical vision for over twenty years. All my work – nine previous books, numerous articles, book chapters, blogs, interviews, classes, lectures and conference presentations – embodies and arises from this timeless and unchanging realization. What is this original revelation? It is the direct experience of the world as divine in substance, form and consciousness. It's all God! Literally. Not the anthropomorphic God created by humans in their likeness, but a living, divine and conscious universe of infinite beauty, love, and flow that we can learn to experience directly and together.

And it's all based on mysticism – the firsthand experience of the sacred – which was humanity's original religion. Upon its central revelations were built numerous world theologies shaped by culture, era, geography and personality, each one a prism refracting the original pantheistic vision into conceptual belief systems. If we want to understand the divine, and particularly if we wish to transform our current human crisis, we must awaken the mystical consciousness of a divine being in a divine world, an experience that becomes increasingly available in sacred aging. Here is a brief tour through my work.

Death of a Hero, Birth of the Soul: Answering the Call of Midlife (1995, 1997)

- The seminal vision for all my work
- Examines the male midlife passage
- Describes the psychological, spiritual and mystical dimensions of the second half of life
- Introduces us to the mystical experience – our original awareness of a living divine reality that underlies all

religion
- Imagines the mystical transformations possible in the second half of life

But Where Is God? Psychotherapy and the Religious Search (1999)

- Conventional psychotherapy completely misses mystical dimension of healing
- This book for counseling professionals outlines the responsible integration of psychotherapy and spirituality
- Presents a profound model of the religious psyche and its spiritual journey

Ordinary Enlightenment: Experiencing God's Presence in Everyday Life (2000)

- Explores the experience of Presence central to the mystical experience: What it is, how can we experience it, and the many ways it transforms our perception of the world
- Introduces the practice of Mystical Consciousness awakening the awareness of God's Presence and the perception of Heaven on Earth

Finding Heaven Here (2009)

- My Doctor of Ministry dissertation
- Engages a chorus of mystic voices all describing the direct perception of Heaven on Earth here and now
- The earlier model of the religious psyche now evolves into a tool for understanding, perceiving, and living in Heaven on Earth (Heaven's Compass)
- Contains exercises for cultivating the mystical experience of Heaven on Earth

The Three Secrets of Aging: A Radical Guide (2012)

- Shares my own mystical experience of aging
- Describes the natural unfolding of mystical consciousness in the aging process
- Outlines the central dynamics of mystical aging: Aging is an initiation into a new dimension of life, a transformation of self and consciousness, and a revelation of a sacred world all around us

Bedtime Stories for Elders: What Fairy Tales Can Teach Us About the New Aging (2012)

- Presents the mystical nature of aging in a fun and symbolic way
- A collection of old and new fairy tales, each an allegory of the transformative dynamics of humanity's new aging
- Journaling questions and experiential exercises help readers discover the meaning of these tales in their own lives

What Aging Men Want: The Odyssey as a Parable of Male Aging (2013)

- Introduces *The Odyssey* as a profound myth of male aging (as Bly's *Iron John* did for midlife men)
- Men grow tired of the patriarchal model of compulsive warrior as they age
- They long to come home to peace, quiet and love, but it's not easy after a lifetime of warrior competition
- Odysseus' adventures on his ten-year journey home symbolize the tasks men face in opening their hearts and coming home from the war

Breakthrough **(2014)**

- Autobiographical novel about a middle-aged psychologist whose life is turned upside down through the mystical experiences of a new client
- Increasingly affected by this client's altered state of consciousness, the psychologist journeys into the realm of divine consciousness and the revolutionary spirituality of aging, revealing possibilities never before imagined

The Divine Human: The Final Transformation of Sacred Aging **(2016)**

- Culminates the journey into mystical aging
- Draws again on the words of the great mystics to describe the coming of a Divine Human in a Divine World
- Adds my own mystical realizations, exercises for experiencing our personal divinity, and the possibilities of sacred action in healing the world
- It lifts the veil on a new kind of humanity and new era of spiritual evolution

About John Robinson

Dr. Robinson is a clinical psychologist with a second doctorate in ministry, an ordained interfaith minister, the author of nine books and numerous articles on the psychology, spirituality and mysticism of the New Aging, and a frequent speaker at Spirituality and Conscious Aging Conferences across the country. You can learn more about his work and schedule at www.johnrobinson.org.

A Message to the Reader

Thank you for purchasing *Mystical Activism*. My sincere hope is that it will awaken in you the profound resources of divine consciousness, mystical problem-solving, transpersonal dialogue, and your own transformation to support your journey through these difficult times and guide your own mystical activism for the enlightenment of humanity. Previous titles in this series amplify most of the subjects addressed and can further energize your spiritual evolution. You are welcome to contact me through my website and, if you found this book helpful, please review it at your favorite online site.

TRANSFORMATION

Transform your life, transform your world - Changemakers
Books publishes for individuals committed to transforming their
lives and transforming the world. Our readers seek to become
positive, powerful agents of change. Changemakers Books
inform, inspire, and provide practical wisdom and skills to
empower us to write the next chapter of humanity's future.
If you have enjoyed this book, why not tell other readers by
posting a review on your preferred book site.

Recent bestsellers from Changemakers Books are:

Integration
The Power of Being Co-Active in Work and Life
Ann Betz, Karen Kimsey-House
Integration examines how we came to be polarized in our dealing
with self and other, and what we can do to move from an either/
or state to a more effective and fulfilling way of being.
Paperback: 978-1-78279-865-1 ebook: 978-1-78279-866-8

Bleating Hearts
The Hidden World of Animal Suffering
Mark Hawthorne
An investigation of how animals are exploited for
entertainment, apparel, research, military weapons, sport, art,
religion, food, and more.
Paperback: 978-1-78099-851-0 ebook: 978-1-78099-850-3

Lead Yourself First!
Indispensable Lessons in Business and in Life
Michelle Ray
Are you ready to become the leader of your own life? Apply
simple, powerful strategies to take charge of yourself, your
career, your destiny.
Paperback: 978-1-78279-703-6 ebook: 978-1-78279-702-9

Burnout to Brilliance
Strategies for Sustainable Success
Jayne Morris
Routinely running on reserves? This book helps you transform
your life from burnout to brilliance with strategies for sustainable
success.
Paperback: 978-1-78279-439-4 ebook: 978-1-78279-438-7

Goddess Calling
Inspirational Messages & Meditations of Sacred Feminine
Liberation Thealogy
Rev. Dr. Karen Tate
A book of messages and meditations using Goddess archetypes
and mythologies, aimed at educating and inspiring those with
the desire to incorporate a feminine face of God into their
spirituality.
Paperback: 978-1-78279-442-4 ebook: 978-1-78279-441-7

The Master Communicator's Handbook
Teresa Erickson, Tim Ward
Discover how to have the most communicative impact in this
guide by professional communicators with over 30 years of
experience advising leaders of global organizations.
Paperback: 978-1-78535-153-2 ebook: 978-1-78535-154-9

Meditation in the Wild
Buddhism's Origin in the Heart of Nature
Charles S. Fisher Ph.D.
A history of Raw Nature as the Buddha's first teacher, inspiring
some followers to retreat there in search of truth.
Paperback: 978-1-78099-692-9 ebook: 978-1-78099-691-2

Ripening Time
Inside Stories for Aging with Grace
Sherry Ruth Anderson
Ripening Time gives us an indispensable guidebook for growing
into the deep places of wisdom as we age.
Paperback: 978-1-78099-963-0 ebook: 978-1-78099-962-3

Striking at the Roots
A Practical Guide to Animal Activism
Mark Hawthorne
A manual for successful animal activism from an author with
first-hand experience speaking out on behalf of animals.
Paperback: 978-1-84694-091-0 ebook: 978-1-84694-653-0

Readers of ebooks can buy or view any of these bestsellers by
clicking on the live link in the title. Most titles are published
in paperback and as an ebook. Paperbacks are available in
traditional bookshops. Both print and ebook formats are available
online.

Find more titles and sign up to our readers' newsletter at
http://www.johnhuntpublishing.com/transformation
Follow us on Facebook at
https://www.facebook.com/Changemakersbooks